Nicky Goodale

KW-481-741

J Marks was born in Los Angeles in 1942, graduated from high school at thirteen, and obtained his Ph.D. at twenty. Since then, he has become a counter-culture legend. His films have won awards, his photos have been shown at leading museums, his articles have appeared in every underground magazine, and his book and record album, *Rock and Other Four Letter Words*, have been bestsellers. J Marks is the pen name for Jamake Mamake Highwater.

J Marks

MICK JAGGER
The Singer, Not the Song

ABACUS edition first published in Great Britain 1974
by Sphere Books Ltd
30/32 Gray's Inn Road, London WC1X 8JL
Copyright © J Marks 1973

For Alta Black
... who told the duck about the swan

ISBN 0 349 12288 1

Set in Monotype Baskerville

*Printed in Great Britain by Cox & Wyman Ltd,
London, Reading and Fakenham*

Acknowledgments

Sharon Edwards was the editor of this book; her teethmarks are visible everywhere in the manuscript. I had wanted to do a fictional memoir about the world of pop. Sharon suggested that I do a long subjective essay about Mick Jagger . . . it turned out being a non-fictional novel.

I am very grateful to Jean Gyory and the Government of Belgium for making it possible for me to write this book in voluntary exile. I also have a debt for inspirations and conversations with David Linker, Jean-Pierre Frayssine . . . and Monique . . . who always turns up as the women in my books. And let me not forget Carol D, house groupie at Max's, who lent so much smack and smut to the narration. I'm grateful too for the fine pictures of Andy Dalton, Ellen Goldberg and Marty Hoffner plus, of course, the classic studies by Marc Sharratt.

The cycle of an idea seems not to have a beginning once it is completed, but I don't ever want to forget that Larry Townsend at the Chicago *Tribune* permitted me to do a long series of profiles when the *atmosphere of fiction* was still considered foreign to journalism. What Townsend started Seymour Peck at *The New York Times* perpetuated when he let me score a litany for Janis Joplin which was unnaturally emotional for the *Times*. The circle was completed when Patrick O'Connor gave me the chance to write this book.

As for the rest of my indebtedness, which the initiated will glimpse between many of the lines, I simply tip my hat. Since I have intended to imagine, compose and orchestrate a work no less derivative than those of Mr Charles Ives, I shall only note that he was the kind of constructive thief who rarely said *thank you* and never said *please*.

J MARKS (Jamake)
Brussels, 1973

Photograph Acknowledgments

The author and publisher would like to thank the following for supplying photographs or for giving permission for their reproduction: Colin Board; Marc Sharratt; Atlantic; Linda Eastman; Rex Features Ltd; Kathy McGowan; S.K.R. Photos; Andy Dalton; and Goldberg-Hoffner. The last section of photographs are taken from the film *Performance* and are reproduced by kind permission of Warner Bros Inc.

'I am a specialist, God help me, in events in inner space and time, in experiences called thoughts, images, reveries, dreams, visions, hallucinations, dreams of memories, memories of dreams, memories of visions, dreams of hallucinations, refractions of refractions of refractions of that original Alpha and Omega of experience and reality ... that Reality on whose repression, denial, splitting, projection, falsification, and general desecration and profanation our civilisation as much as on anything is based'

R. D. LAING
The Politics of Experience

Through the Past Darkly

He is rather small. Sitting side-saddle in a straightback chair, his hairy head resting against the cold tiled wall as professional hands fashion a face for him. An intonation of purple on his hooded lids. A careful Egyptian signature around his eyes.

He is rather thin. Sitting quietly amidst the persistent clamour. A rumpled robe is pulled over his spectacular silver jumpsuit. He continues to stare at the ceiling when the make-up man murmurs something to him. 'Farfuckinout . . .' he laughs.

He has a rather extraordinary Mouth. There is something conspicuously naked about his lips. Liquid, languid, large. 'We could swing all over the place on a rope,' this exceptional Mouth says, though the face remains motionless beneath the constantly moving hands of the make-up artist.

'Well, maybe *you* could,' someone says.

'I would,' the Mouth answers simply.

'I know,' someone grins.

He is rather quiet now. His narrow shoulders pulled inward as his small fingers fondle an imaginary cameo at his throat. Bette Davis-style. He sits patiently as the cosmetic transformation also alters his sex. As he becomes a retouched reality. Or more precisely, as one reality becomes another. Finally *he is what he wasn't*. And the make-up man smiles and dusts off his shoulders.

His name is Mick Jagger. He's a star.

Another youth sits before his mirror, surrounded by equal clamour, but a commotion of a more treble timbre. He's tall and skinny, flat chested and so white and so smooth that it seems that his flesh is supported by a down-quilt rather than a musculature.

His hands fly through the air like hummingbirds. A motion so precise, dainty and rapid that it borders on effeminate science fiction. The target of these darting digits is a mountain of cosmetics which spreads before him like a dragon's dinner. A banquet of vials, pots and tubes, greases, liquids, sticks and cakes of colour. He devours these sumptuously, twisting them around his eyes and lips, polishing his cheeks with them, and raising a cloud of pale pinkness with his powerful powderpuff.

His large housewife-mouth contorts kinesthetically as he glues artificial eyelashes into place, leaning back now and batting these new butterfly-eyes with satisfaction.

He has a rather cruel mouth. There is something conspicuously obscene about his flat lips. It's a muscular mouth, made wide and absolutely horizontal by the exercise of viciousness. It is a mouth poised for retaliation. Vigorous, venomous, violent. 'I'm taking my tits and getting front row seats, my dear, even if it means going with that old fart with the hennaed toupee,' this mean mouth says, though the face remains motionless beneath his constantly moving hands.

'Just your luck if he's wearing jockeys the night you get your smart seats,' someone says.

'He's an *artiste*, my dear, you seem to forget that he is a *very great artiste*,' the mouth answers.

'He's a faggot,' someone grins.

'Look . . . Miss Bitch,' the mouth strikes back with a tiny shower of spittle on the *BBBBBitch*. 'Elvis may be a lady . . . and Rock may be a princess, but Mick Jagger, my dear, is a MAN, and you'd better believe it.'

He is quiet now. His narrow shoulders pulled inward as his long painted fingernails adjust his chandeliers. Bette Davis-style. He pulls on a tulle number, tiered and pearled, like a pair of jeans, zipping up and scratching his ass. Back before the mirror, he has become a retouched reality. Or more precisely, he has become what he thinks he is. His name is Rita. He's a star.

'*What a drag it is getting old*,' Rita intones as he heads for the stage.

On the street you can get layed, replayed and parlayed for a pair of tickets. 'Every energy freak in town's gonna turn out to see them. I mean, it's fuckinincredible, that's what it is man.'

A lean girl with hair which looks like an unsuccessful electrocution strolls past in a continuous torrent of tears. She's eating a slice of pizza between the sobs. 'Dudes are takin' other dudes,' she cries. 'I mean it's *unnatural*.'

While backstage at the Garden the Mick makes a declaration: 'It's absurd to assume that I have any special control over the audience. I don't. I don't even think about it.' He smiles the Jagger smile, announcing his victory march to age thirty by the deep ridges which frame his Mouth. These tracks testify to the fact that perpetual adolescence is rapidly going out of vogue as an hysterical life-style. After ten years, Mick has gotten his tits together. Like Marilyn, he's matured into a unique beauty. Thing is, Mick uses everything he's got and that's quite a lot. He purses his lips and lays his hand on his hip before he hikes up ihis pants to display the commodity he has packaged so well in tight white pants.

A lady journalist rolls her eyes. A large stagehand pretends not to notice. And a nineteen-year-old, blue-eyed stock clerk shakes his head dramatically over a hamburger sixteen miles away, and tells his girlfriend very softly, 'Jesus, honey, I'd sure love to ball Mick Jagger.'

Somebody's mother exclaims that 'he's just plain embarrassing'. And her son agonises: 'Aw, ma, that's not where it's at.'

As for Mick, he splashes on some fragrance and checks his eyeliner with his pinkie.

Then suddenly he lifts his head – listening. Like a deer. Sniffing the air. For the first time, through the indefinable roar of the dressing room, comes the harrowingly serious, living-breathing-sound of the AUDIENCE. You can hear it with that intense dimensionality of music on stoned ears.

A visual sound. You can smell it. For Jagger it's the whistling of a kettle. *It's time.* A casual indication in a familiar world. For everyone else it sounds like a hungry universe: a presence so keyed and complex and enormous that it is simply impossible to imagine stepping wilfully out into it. Pitting your loneness against its massiveness.

But Jagger's eyes flash not like the matador but like the bull. Kicking in the stall. As he approaches the resonance of blinding light and blistering sound, he *blooms*. Like a Japanese fan. Multiple auras, geysering from him in successive waves. You can see the active force with which he will catalyse this mammoth assembly into a Wagnerian orchestra performing the intricate notes of his ritual music.

DARKNESS. A succession of hurried words. Then the short single bombardment of the introduction, rocketing back and forth in the dark. *Lights*. And – Lord – the *wailllllllllllll* of the whole fucking universe.

When you open your eyes he's out there. In the heat of the sun. Blinding radiance. Boogieing. Squirming like a butterfly stuck with a pin. *Bull with butterfly wings*. He's a Babylonian deity . . . he's Mick Jagger . . . he's a star.

THE PSYCHODRAMA OF THE HUNG MAN

'Ya don't want me pants tah fall down, now do ya?'

You really don't have time to speculate about alternatives when you're always the centre of attention, I said to David D. in his New York loft which lingered somewhere between an existence as a factory and as a refurbished artist's pad, like a huge truck stalled on a long hill. Its ribs, tubes and wires are nude from the waist up. Over-sized washers, refrigerators and driers stand around self-consciously like the first guests to arrive at a party. David himself staggers around in a Thrift Shop robe, his face red and wrinkled from a long conversation with a pillow. He keeps grunting *yeah* as he shuffles blindly in the direction of his cup of coffee. *It's a questionable aspect of stardom*, I said nodding to his old lady who kept piling my plate with eight-pound steamed clams. *It's a way of living that's totally unfulfilled by lots of personalities who simply lack the stuff to fill a life which has the tension and the demand for fresh material of a stand-up routine. You know what I mean?*

David D. was wiping the sleep from his perfectly round eyes. He didn't respond, but pushed his nose between the two hard, white, open lips of an enormous clam and sucked out the musky meat. His old lady's plate was very white and empty as she continuously marched between the stove topped with boiling pots and the table topped with the skeletons of twenty-seven abandoned and herculean clams. Next came tortillas and chili con carne.

Jagger, however, measures up to the role, I told David. *He's continually in the centre – all questions and answers are conveyed to and through him. If he is not directly in the heart of a discussion, people automatically fill him in on what's been said. Without any noticeable ceremony, doors are opened for him. People let him walk in front of them. Not just because he's a star – that kind of behaviour prevails only with the upstarts who have momentarily risen above groupiedom – but because Jagger has this notion about himself which has a powerful impact on every moment of his life. That he is special. He thinks it and so it's true. It's really true. It's true because Mick thinks it and because we think it and nobody's ever going to really know which came first.*

(When you're always the centre of attention you do most of your thinking while you're talking. You don't have much of a facility for self-examination because you're always being asked questions by others before you ask anything of yourself. Besides, everything you think – your favourite ice cream to your religious convictions – is given the same importance. And even your relationships are based on something other than friendship: you are in a privileged position in which you don't have time to be lonely and therefore you don't need to seek affection. Your friends are almost indistinct from your fans. It's really doubtful that you ever trust anyone. Everyone pursues your attention and so you pursue no-one. Everyone watches you and you begin to find that you are so busy watching yourself being watched that you never make the effort to look at anyone else. The people you do notice are simply the people who give you some exceptional kind of attention. Of the thousands who constantly try to get your notice, you focus perhaps on ten or fifteen – a reaction rather than an action. And though you get terrifically bored and passively search for a disguise that will give you a safe and momentary anonymity, you always carry your stardom with you. Playing at being ordinary with every inordinate device in your reach. Writing songs at four in the morning. Taking a tough tumble which immediately changes from experience into the lyrics for a song. And you begin to suspect that most of what you do is done so you will have something to write about, material for your ravenous, self-expressive appetite. You don't separate the act of writing a lyric about somebody from the reality of the person. They become elements of each other. And gradually your performance merges with your existence. You cannot tell the dancer from the dance.)

David, I said, flopping down on the bulbous corpse of an overstuffed chair, *Mick does everything – even drinking a glass of wine at home alone – as if it were a medium close-up. As if it were a performance.*

David D. belched lavishly and wiped his mouth with the back of his hand. 'Put that in your book,' he grunted. And then: 'Do you know that we ate sixty-seven of those clams last night,' he said slowly.

The question, really, is what does Mick Jagger think about when he jerks off. Answer that and you've got a book.

When the six arclights rebound off the scarf-tussled body of the Mick there is an instantaneous event. A community is born. Jagger becomes the fragile focus of a massive energy, the delicate instrument which transmits the stupendous force of the audience and returns it in a rarified performance of active powers. Twenty thousand mouths roar at a twelve-foot stage which has been prefabricated at one end of a boundless ice-skating palace in Vancouver. The sound turns Jagger's muscular generators. He lays his hand on the microphone and leans toward it like a lover. Closing his eyes slowly.

He puts his cheek against it and opens his lubricious Mouth and begins to yowl . . . snorting with the ballsy gutturalese of a black bull bomber. . . . *gooooldcoast sssslave 'ip bound for cooooottonfeeelds*. . . . *Aaah, brooown suuuugar, how cum you taaaste so gud?*

As the sound filters out over the mob which covers every surface and rebounds beyond the walls of the arena, the rioting outside slowly fades out, and bloodied policemen are carted off to the hospital like blue, overstuffed pillows. While along the edge of the platform Botticelli-seraphim gaze radiantly with smiles and tears. 'Man,' somebody is moaning, 'I'm just plain blown away . . . my God Mick, but you're just so fuckin' *stone gorgeous!*'

When the Stones get to 'Rocks Off' two guys come flying over the stands in back of the platform, barely touching the ground as some weird sort of violent energy propels them like madmen, screaming all the while: 'Chickenshiiiiit-mutter-fuck-cops!' Their seizure continues as they fly around and uproot some railings that run down the stands and manage to dump them over the side. The sound as they crash on the concrete is heard over the magnanimous amplitude of the music. 'Cocksuuucker-sonnovabeeeech!' Until some ushers tackle one of the guys and start giving him a ferocious work-over. The other one gets away but comes back like a maniac. And while the ushers are busy pummeling his friend, he starts kicking at one of them, splitting open his face and releasing a theatrical flood of blood.

Meanwhile way in the back where Mick is barely visible, kids buck, bob and boogie as if this exceptional live event were just another Saturday record-hop at the local high school. There is no mob, only individual faces which make happy contact with each other. Blonde kids with hair down to their waists and kids with beards. Girls with glasses and outrageous freaks from 1967 alongside student body presidents and members of the Scholarship Society. Jocks and ten-year-olds with their stoic, dry-mouthed parents. And also kids who look scared. Who sit very still, clenching their nylon jackets in damp hands and watch hypnotically with enormous eyes.

Out of time, somehow, they are out of time and afraid to show what they feel. But *loving* it all, even loving being scared out of their skulls.

'He's what it's all about,' seventeen-year-old Dudley Wolfe is explaining patiently. 'I mean, he's Mick Jagger, y'know, and he's so fucking amazing, man. Like, I'd just like to be able to be like that for ten minutes. Just ten minutes to be that cool. I mean, like, there's just nobody like Mick. He's such *class*, man, such a fucking heavy trip, y'know.'

'Jagger?' says this L.A.-type surfing-freak, hardly moving his lips and keeping a steel glint steadily focused in his unfurnished eyes. 'Dig it, mister, it's big-shit-Jagger, right? He's some kind of a trip, right? He's got this ritzy lady with tits and he's filthy rich and somebody laid this swank house in the south of France on him, right? I mean, man, he's Big Jumpin' Jack Shit Himself, and I'd like to get the muther. I mean cut him, man . . .' and the light in his grey eyes goes purple and sexy, '. . . I mean, like, hurt his ass bad.' Then he turns back to stare at the stage, pushing both his hands into his groin and hunching over, never losing his hold on the flagrantly prancing figure down there in the hot lights.

He's alone. He has come to the concert by himself. He's come all the way from San Diego, following the caravan at a distance. Never approaching. Charlotte Corday with a California tan. The dagger between his legs. Raging amorously as he mouths the songs, never missing a word. An assassin with a hard-on . . . the most frightening of animals sick with love. Troubled in his large body, which houses a delicate obsession, clenched between his fingers like a lace handkerchief. Agonised by this androgynous beauty whom he follows at a distance. In rage. In heat. Passionately destructive. Mick, watch out! *Jeest as ev'ry cop is a criminal and all the sinners saints . . . as heads is tails . . . jeeest call me Lu-ci-fer . . . cuz I'm in need of summm restrainttttt.* His name is Dominique R. He's a killer.

Two guitars and one hour and forty minutes later, Mick collapses in a liquid heap in the dressing room. The glitter has been washed from his chest by sweat. His make-up is smeared and his hair is matted. But his energies seem undepleted: 'For us, the first one is always a dress rehearsal,' he says. 'The audience can force you to give a great performance. It's happened to us before. In Liverpool ... we were shit. But we pulled it up and did a fantastic second show.' Somebody says something lame about how beautifully Mick controls the audience: wide-eyed flattery No. 3. 'I don't go for all that crap about control,' Jagger explains flatly. 'All these people always saying, "Oh, I saw Elvis in Madison Square Garden and he was in total control of the audience." I don't believe any audience is under control unless you've got them policed by your own police. I don't profess to be in control of the audience, and I don't believe they think I am. You're in some sort of control – say, fifty percent, kinda. but you're not ever in total command.' And he falls back and rests his head against the wall. His daily dose of vitamins, protein pills and bean curd just barely keeps him afloat once he starts to come down from the adrenalin of performance. He suddenly cracks into the Jagger smile for no apparent reason and closes his eyes very slowly.

Buzzzzzzzzzzzzzzzzzzzzzzzzzzzzzzzzzzzzzzzz . . . Operator?

Bonjour, monsieur, quel numéro demandez-vous, s'il vous plaît?

Oui, oui, operator, est-ce que c'est possible en anglais, s'il vous plaît?

Quel numéro demandez-vous, s'il vous plaît? C'est le service international.

Oui, oui, mais est-ce que vous parlez anglais, madame? C'est impossible en français.

Yez, a leetle beet.

Well, thank God for that! Operator, I'm trying to reach a town in Wales.

Wut iz de nom of zee zity, pleaz?

It's called Rod-nor-shire, Rodnorshire . . . and . . .

Could you pleaz spelling siz nom, seer?

. . . uh, sure, operator . . . it's spelled R-O-D-N-O-R-S-H-I-R-E.

Rodnorshire, oui? In Wales?

17

Yah, that's right operator. And the area code is 05-47-81.
Un moment, s'il vous plaît...
...
...
...
.... yez, sir? Are you dere?
Yes, operator.
To reached dat numéro in Wales, zir, you may dial automatique...
No, no, madame, pas automatique ...
*... by firz dialing 951 and you den waiting for zee internationale
musique, comprenez-vous? .... and den you dialing zee area code
44 and den 5, 47 and 81, following immediate by zee tree digit
numéro. Comprenez-vous, monsieur?*
*No, no, operator .... I just tried that and it doesn't work. I
dialled 951 and that operator told me that the number is not automatic
and that I had to place the call with you.*
Un moment, s'il vous plaît...
...
...
...
...
...
...
...
...
...
...
...
....
Operator, are you there?
...
...
...
...
.. click-click
O god, please don't hang up! Operator!
...
...

. . . .
. . . . *yez zir? Are you dere?*

YES, OPERATOR! Is that you?

Monsieur, what iz zeh city you are try to reaching, s'il vous plaît?

I told you, operator, it's Rodnorshire: R/O/D/N/O/R/S/H/I/R/E in Wales. The area code is 05-47-81.

Un moment, si'l vous plaît. . . . .
. . . .
. . . .
. . . .*yez, zir, are you still dere? We haff the operature in Wales on deh line.*

Thiiiiis is the operator, may I assist you sirh?

Operator?

Thiiiiis is the operator, sirh, may I assist you?

I'm trying to reach Alexis Korner at his home in Wales. The area code is 05-47-81. And the number . . .

In what city in Wales is that residence located, sirh?

I think it's in Rodnorshire . . . but . . .

One moment, sirh. . . . .
. . . .
. . . .*there is no such city in Wales, sirh.*

Wait a second, operator, don't hang up. . . . I have another name somewhere. Hold on a second. . . . Don't hang up . . . here . . . here it is, operator. Could it be L-L-A-N-G-U-N-L-L-O? Is that possible?

One moment, if you please. . . . .
. . . .*yes, sir, that area code checks with that town in Wales. If you will wait just one moment, I will get that number on the line for you.*

Well, thank god for that.

BuzzzzzzzzzzzzzClickkkkkkkkk . . . uzzzzzzzzzz. . . . .
. . . . .click. . . . .
. . . . .click. . . . . HELLO?   Hello?

Alexis? Is that you?

Yes, yes. Who is this please?

It's Jamake. I'm calling from Brussels.

What in hell's name are you doing in Brussels?

19

Precisely . . . . *I want to talk to you about Mick
Jagger.*
I know. Phillip told me you were going to call.
Do you have time to talk about it now?
Sure, why not.
Where should we start?

Michael Philip Jagger. Five feet, eight inches. Ten stones, six pounds. Blue eyes. Brown hair. Born in Dartford, one of the oversaturated suburbs of sprawling London, on July 26, 1943 . . . to Joe and Eva Jagger. Michael's father Joe was a physical training instructor. A man with a stocky, well-made body which he tended like a prize horse. His ruggedness however was superficial, and his intelligence and gentility helped him climb to the position of senior lecturer in physical education. Mick, with his younger brother, Christopher, grew up in a middle-class home in which there was no interest in music. His primary education at Maypole County School was unimpressive.

'I guess you realise,' Alexis Korner says with his handsomely correct diction, 'that Keith Richards and Mick were friends for a short time when they were very young.'

Keith was a half-pint with a huge head, protruding ears, and a rare smile. Mick and this serious little dwarf often raced around the grounds of that primitive school in Wilmington, Kent, throwing up a cloud of dust in which their identities were momentarily mixed. 'It's strange,' Keith remembers, 'we used to hang out together, y'know. But then I moved and didn't see him for a long time. That's when we were maybe five, six or seven.'

'As a kid,' Mick recalls, 'we lived quite happily. I wasn't very passionate about school in those days . . . but who was? The war was over but naturally it left very little impression on me. I dunno . . . I suppose the only thing I really remember was my mum, y'know, taking down the blankets from the windows when the blackouts and the fighting were over.'

Before he went off to Wentworth County Primary School, Mick saw Keith once again. 'I once met him,' Keith recalls, 'selling ice creams outside the public library. I bought one.' Then he moved away and they didn't see each other for a long time.

En route from the Wentworth School to the Dartford Grammar School, Mick managed to lose his school cap often enough to express his disgust for wearing a school uniform. 'It was a drag . . . all that peaked cap stuff.' Naturally it was a bit awkward to be the son of a teacher. You were always expected to come up with more than your fellow students, but the Mick was resolute about his independence. 'My dad's job really didn't rub off on me. I didn't believe in racing if there was a good chance of walking. Even now, y'know, organised games are hardly my cup. You wouldn't catch me going to a football match.' He was too delicate and devilish for the sporting life. 'Now I didn't really mind having a go at basketball . . . but there was also the little matter of tackling in Rugby. Well, enough is enough . . . that's a tough sport and in most of the games somebody got bashed and I hated it.'

Those were the 1940s days of John Wayne and Teddy Boy Brando, when Ray Bradbury had written a short story about a man who committed himself to the playground for four years so that his son could be spared the horrors and humiliations. There was no place in the world of the playground for a future pop star with delicate hands and an inclination to be emotional. 'When I couldn't get out of it, I'd try to keep out of the way of the ball, y'know, figuring that I couldn't get hurt if I didn't do more than run all over the place. It was a real drag when somebody passed me the ball.'

What terrified Mick was not only the discipline of sports but also the bravado and masculine competition. But his father didn't recognise the fact that sports intimidated his son. 'Mick had a natural agility. It's hard to say now, of course, but I feel that if he had had a different temperament he could have been a really great athlete.' The same could be said about Marie Antoinette.

What excited young Jagger's imagination was the theatricality of history. He liked history lessons, and found himself transported from middle-class England to times of lavish costumes and surrealistic elegance. In history he found drama. In sports he found cruelty. Language arts also amused him although he was, like most budding artists, hardly at the top of his class academically. But he was good at French and English.

At fifteen Mick had already discovered music. It wasn't the sort of music which was encouraged at grammar schools in traditional England. 'What do you get out of that goo-gee woe-gee music?' his music teacher demanded. But of course, Mick could not explain. He could not tell them that it was the secret beating heart of AMERICA – a magic land like the lands in his history books. A land in which the streets were paved in gold and huge, shiny black men danced through the cotton fields in spectacular production numbers staged by Busby Berkeley. Heading for the gym to the sock-hop ball where *the joint is really jumpin' and the cats are goin' wild and the music really flips me and y'dig my crazy style! I'm ready, Ready/ Ready/Teddy/I'm ready, wooooooh!* Little Richard holding hands in the back seat with Bobby Troup. *Won't you get hip to this kindly tip, an' take that Califoooornia trip . . . get your kicks' on Route Sixty-Sixxxxxx.*

These jubilant sounds . . . Bo and Chuck and Little R. . . . transporting him. Releasing him from a boy's body. Lifting him from everything mundane and petty and practic-cal. This rich black Teutonic symphony. With its gigantic abandon and rhythmic ecstasy. Rocking everything in sight. Sounds rising magically from a platter like the genie from the lamp. Working absolute miracles for him. Releasing the high tension of his body which needed an arena, but not a play-ground. Not a sports field. Shaking him profoundly with huge, violent throbs of creative energy. Not brutality. But confirming everything, even the most dismal suffering. Confirming even his childhood. Putting this perfect cry of outrage in his throat though he could not yet pronounce it. Making him feel exceptional. Physical. Sexual. Plausible.

After the last note died away, he looked up and he was fifteen and it was nearly time for him to take his GCE examinations and his music teacher asked him: 'What do you get out of that boo-gee woe-gee music?'

'I don't think that Mick was a very happy kid,' Alexis Korner says softly.

'No,' I mutter, suddenly losing sight of the image of the young Mick, 'I think it's terrifying to be different.'

Rita is not well. When he had rolled over on the floor-bound mattress which is the centrepiece of his junk-eloquen boudoir, selectively furnished from the debris of the pavements of New York, he had complained to his Puerto Rican lover that he was not well. His teeth, he said, were like four dozen vicious queens, nagging him day and night.

'Paco,' he shouts through his enormous mouth, as he slithers into deep magenta tights and an antique frock he had borrowed from Jackie, 'why the hell don't you answer when I'm talking to you.' But Paco has slipped out with the five bucks Rita had hidden under the stately white stall shower which stands in the middle of the eight by six kitchen. 'Cocksucker,' he mutters as he puts a pot of water on the three-burner and dumps two heaps of instant Maxwell into his favourite Bloomingdale mug. 'Sonabitch *spick* mutherfuck'' he enunciates slowly as he grimaces in the mirror and spits up a walloping wad of mucus, the color of Helena Rubenstein's *Midnight Adventure*. He pulls back his jaws like a vet perusing a mare's mouth and lets out a little cry. 'Look at that would you,' he says impatiently to the face in the mirror. 'How can a girl look her best when her fuckin' mouth is a goddamn slum! I tell you, Mary Jane, it ain't easy when you're a beauty.' And he laughs self-consciously and fills his cup with boiling water.

Now, as he balances a small mirror on the kitchen table he goes to work on his broad, coarse face, gulping occasionally from the coffee mug and hugging the telephone receiver under his chin. He tells a girlfriend all about it. 'That bastard ran off with my last fin,' he says to the telephone. 'Can you believe that spick . . . I mean, my dear, what is a poor girl to do?' And he rolls his eyes and stretches his lips into a mock

23

Monroe smile as if the whole world were a movie set and Andy's camera were constantly rolling somewhere in the wings.

'There's only one thing I want from that muther and that's a pair of seats for opening night. No, *opening night*, my dear that's the only way to fly. You bet your sweet tits it is. Well, like I said, he knows somebody. God knows how or who or when, but he knows *somebody* with the tour. Somebody connected with Peter Rudge or Madison Square Garden or Queen Elizabeth. Probably somebody he screwed one of those long nights when he told me he was scoring a john. But I don't care how or whoever – I just want two seats in the first row centre right under Miss Jagger's lovely loins. And I don't care how I get them. So if you hear anything, tell me tonight when I see you at Max's. Of course I'll be there, my dear child! Do I ever miss an *entrance?*' And he lights a cigarette. 'No . . . I can't. I have a rehearsal and I haven't even opened the fuckin' script. My dear, it's not what they say it is to be a famous movie star. In fact, at times it's shit.' And Rita laughs.

When he hangs up he opens the script and begins to read aloud in transvestite tranquillity. He glances into the mirror and takes another look at his rancid teeth. There are only *two* things he really wants when he makes it big in the movies:

1. To get his teeth capped
2. To travel extensively in Europe and stay at the *best* hotels
3. To get his name legally changed
4. To buy a fabulous collection of antique clothes
5. To get a decent apartment somewhere nice like, maybe, Sutton Place South
6. To get a miniature white poodle, dyed pink
7. To send his mother a mink stole
8. To give maybe five thousand dollars to the Jewish Relief Fund
9. To get rid of that sonabitch spick bastard who keeps ruining my life, dear God, and please help me to find somebody who loves me

24

The Seattle police smile and answer questions politely. Only their dry lips and clenched hands give them away. There is a slow pulse visible in the throat of one bull who keeps his hands locked behind his back. The cops assemble in small groups, totally perhaps one hundred, around the arena which stands near the Space Needle – part of the archi-tectural fantasy composed of parks, fountains and convention halls which was built for the Seattle World's Fair of 1959. At the front door the shakedown goes on quietly: coming up with minor vices (beer, wine and a couple of unorthodox pills) and a few symbols of holocaust, like the .25 automatic special taken from a tall boy with the face of a cocker spaniel.

This weapon is passed silently among the policemen, who gaze upon it. 'That's what this Jagger is all about,' a strapping blond with transparent pink ears confides, 'violence . . .' He says it slowly. 'Jagger comes on stage and makes trouble for kids who normally have a dance and a malt and a good time. That music of theirs is *primitive*. I mean, it's geared to get these kids all worked up and turn them into a mob. That's the only reason we frown on these events. If it were good clean fun or something like that, well, it would be another story. But lots of these kids come here with a chip on their shoulders. They're looking for a fight. And, y'know, we're no dummies. If they start trouble, mister, they gonna get it.' There is a slow pulse visible in his throat and a cautious sexuality behind his unlighted eyes as he slowly rubs the knuckles of his right hand.

Now Mick Jagger smiles down on Seattle like a hobo moon: an aristocratic and luminous beggar king, flapping his shining white rags. He pumps up the enthusiasm of his cloudless audience, ascending into their awed midst. 'Who go free today?' he shouts. 'Angela Davis go free today . . . fuckin' great.'

But if you have to fight, please take your troubles out the door . . . and now I say with sorrow until this time tomorrow, ohhh, we'll bid you all a fond adieu. On with the show . . .

(Several hundred miles south, in San Francisco – guardian

25

of radical chic and the Tammany Hall of political poseurs – they take deliberate note of the events. Several permanent-press Jeremiahs wash their hands in the daily press but somehow the world does not come to an end.)

The second show in Seattle outdistances the warrior mentality in the streets. 'All right now, Seattle, all *right!*' There's an inflection of contempt in Mick's diction but nobody notices. The super-troupers blow their incandescent beams at the stage and Mick Jagger slinks into the mouths of two Gothic serpents painted on the pearly floor. The kids are on their feet, raising a howl you can hear for blocks, and Keith lays on the chords of 'Brown Sugar'.

Fuckinfarout, the Stones is here! Back home in Seattle where the fast dances on Saturday night at the VFW hops are polkas, Yahooooo! And don't they ever look fine. With ole Keither blaaaming away at it. Wyman with his Fender like a rifle at his hip, posed in a diminutive trance. Mick-the-Taylor leaning studiously over his Gibson, looking stupendously clean-cut and innocent beside his fellow-Stones. And Charley-my-boy ticking time on the high hat just as pretty as you please. While the cluckcluck-cluckin-mutherfuckin little red gooser his-self struts his pretty little ass all over the place. Lord, ain't that nice!

A huge, sixteen by forty foot series of mirrors are hung in front of the stage, up above the platform. These shining surfaces bounce the six follow-spots all over the place, providing backlighting and front spotlighting by some weird principle of reflection. Nice trick – the brainchild of Chip Monck who does the sleight-of-hand act which results in the exceptional lighting and production of the Stone's tour.

The mirrors are put together for each show, an assembly of eleven featherweight panels of high-key, coated mylar. As well as being a high-class mirror freak, Monck is a demon in the sound department – each side of the stage is flanked by a hydraulic lift crammed with Tychobrahe speakers. Enough to blow your head off at close range. Each hydraulic shaft weighs in at ten thousand pounds when fully loaded and elevated to a height of eighteen feet, where the sound can fan out and inundate even the most gigantic spaces.

The stage floor, where Mick does all his fancy prancing, is sectional so it can be struck and loaded into trucks and carted off to the next gig. It's made up of six white plywood and Dualon panels on which two bright green fire-breathing dragons are tattooed. They wash the surface down with warm water and Seven-Up to make it truckable and struttable for dancing Mick. Reportedly the demon dragons are a rip-off from a 1940s Donald Duck comic book – from the ferocious pen and paranoia of Walt Disney.

After 'Brown Sugar', Mick veers immediately into 'Bitch' and 'Rocks Off', catching the kids off-guard, not giving them a minute to speculate about the avalanche which is descending upon them. Cachugga-Chugga-Blaaam! A steady bombardment with three direct hits within the first eleven minutes. It's going to be a killer. You can see it in Mick's eyes as the sweat starts. As the first ten rows fondle the horny space between their bodies and his – slowly, slowly turning Jagger on. He responds with a moan and then bares his hips to the boys and girls in the third row. A young guy with the face of a Genet inmate – Divine, the killer – is clutching his harmonica and hurls himself against the stage. His eyes see through the arms which restrain him, glued to Jagger. 'Awww, man,' he screams bountifully, like a love song, 'you gotta let me blow with Mick! You gotta let me do the gig with Mick!' As they lead him off the stage you can see the tears in his eyes. He keeps twisting his head and looking back at Mick, hoping that perhaps their eyes will meet for a second. But Jagger dances on to his own music, as impervious and remote as the god Pan. Building a colossal crescendo with 'Gimme Shelter' – revving straight up into the line: *Ohhhh, childon, it' z jest a shot awaaaay, a shot-away, a shotta-way!* While Taylor's muscular guitar spins a knubby web around Jagger's body. The tune ends with Keith swooping back into the amps only to recover almost immediately, his lips puckered at the mike for the opening of 'Happy' which

27

Mick joins, his tongue at the corner of his moist Mouth. *Bay-baaaay, ah won't ya maka-me hapaaayyy!*

'Tumblin' Dice' slowing down into some additional foreplay . . . something kinda moody. 'Gonna do a blues fer ya now,' Jagger murmurs, as they slip into 'Love In Vain'. In the slow drag, while Charlie spins his drumsticks waiting on the first chorus, Jagger sweats slowly. His workshirt gradually turns dark and rivulets circle falteringly from his hairline

When Mick moistens his Mouth and uvulates drowsily, putting the harp to his Lips and blowing soft and sweet, a girl with freckles and a joint in her hand leans forward and closes her eyes. *Sweet Virginia . . . sweet, sweet, sweet Virgiiiiina.* The delicate ape with profoundly human eyes, almost homo sapien but lingeringly animal: singing ah so sweet and low.

'Yah, that's right,' he mutters without looking up, 'I said *Dominique*. Like, that's my name, man, y'dig?'

'Didn't I see you in L.A.? I mean, I think I talked to you in Los Angeles or maybe it was Vancouver. . . .'

'It happens,' he mutters, a funny grin coming to the edges of his mouth. But still he won't look me in the eye. 'I hang out in lots of towns, y'know. . . .'

'O yah . . .' I say, finally recalling his sullen verbal attack on Jagger in the arena at Vancouver when I was collecting words in the whirling electronic net of my casette recorder. But I decide against telling him that I'm hip to his weird scene.

He shoots a quick glance at me, and I'm suddenly struck by his baby-mouth. I hadn't noticed that before – I was so hung up on the terrible vacancy of his grey eyes. 'You know this fancy *monkey*, this Jagger very well?' he asks. 'I mean, like, are you one of his buddies or something like that?'

'No,' I say.

'. . . like, one of the privileged few,' he laughs unpleasantly. 'Or are you just one of these fuckin' garbage collectors who hangs out with these *superstars* and all that shit.' I say nothing. So he stares at me as if his insult has given him the edge he needs. He sits up straight and turns his head slowly from side to side. It's an extraordinary movement: like an entranced rhinoceros warming up its engine. But now that I have seen his baby-mouth, he no longer frightens me. I begin to see the pathetic outline of the boy trapped behind his man's face. Dying little by little. Turned inside out and convoluted, pacing between identities like a somnambulist, held together only by the violent centrifugal force which emanates from his groin. An angry hunger. *A soft implosion.* Succubus on a surf-board. But otherwise disguised as a California dude. 'So tell me, Dominique,' I say as fraternally as I can, 'where do you come from, huh, and how come you're such a regular at Stones' concerts?'

He just nods his head almost imperceptibly for a while, looking me up and down with as much contempt as he can muster. And that's quite a bit. Then he stands up and tucks in his T-shirt and yawns. Stretching with lavish showmanship. Smirking as he momentarily fondles his groin.

Then he walks away.

I watch after him for a minute, certain that he'll look back to check out my reaction. But he doesn't. I figure I'll see him again.

THE PROLEGOMENON FOR A THEATRE OF TEEN-AGE METAPHYSICS

Mick Jagger represents the most tenacious, wiry, abrasive, rampageous, impetuous, rampant, immitigable, ruffianly, onerous and puzzling aspect of rock 'n' roll, I said through the door to David D. who was in the can.

'The Stones, man,' he grunted, 'is the toughest fuckin' band alive.'

The toughest music-makers, I quoted slowly while I thought ahead, trying to figure how such diverse characteristics could successfully span more than a decade. *The epitome of punkiness, there's no question about that*, I told David while I paced the full length of the loft, going to the window and looking out at the blank wall on the opposite side of the narrow light-well. *A really punk mentality. You can identify it easily when Iggy Stooge does a bad imitation of the same quality – but in Jagger it's much*

29

harder to put your finger on it. I mean, you can't quite figure out how he does it. Y'know what I mean? At which point Andy wandered in, looking lost as usual. I nodded to her.

'Are you actually going to see Jagger in London?' she asked with that concealed smile which always accompanied anything remotely connected with Mick.

I don't know, I said.

'Well,' she intoned like a cat, circling me with that incredible body, 'if you do see him do you think you'll show him the photographs I took?'

Ah, tall, clean, lean and deep beige Andy. What a fuckin' teen-age queen! Her incomparable, muscular midriff disappearing into her sheer pants just hairs above the junction of her groin. Unselfconsciously low on her hips, low enough so you could see the perfect plastic contour of her beautiful bony pelvis and that marvelously sleek flesh, flagrantly punctuated by her perfectly oval navel. Yes, indeed. A Modigliani with a perpetual heat. Mainly for Mick. Geometrical pears upon her chest, barely breasts but O so sweet.

'Would you like him to see your photos?' I asked.

Ah, tall, clean, lean and deeply tanned – wild Andora. What a dream. Dark Dresden shoulders, fragile as ceramic. Long legs and arms and burnished honey hair down to there. Her leg thrown over the arm of a chair like a boy and her fingers working ever so delicately on her long throat while she pondered my question.

'Well,' she muttered with the kind of post-hippie cool that borders on lifelessness . . . traces of ennui, 'do what you want.' And then she handed me a copy of the cover photograph and told me to take it along . . . just in case. 'You never can tell,' she said slowly, her weird, clear eyes never leaving mine. And then she flashed a happy embarrassment and left the room. That was just about the same moment that David made his re-entrance, buckling up and prancing like a cat just out of the sandbox.

'The toughest fuckin' band alive . . .' he said again, playing a tune on his unplugged IBM Selectric Typewriter and then dropping into a big chair and thinking hard.

Paragonian punks. An overdose of narcissism bordering on perversity. Comradeship of Wagnerian dimensions ... Siegmund and Sieglinda straining an innocent incestuousness to its utter limits. Abject Midas cynicism. Everything they touch turns to shit and gold. But it takes time! Theirs is no easy alchemy.

Plus of course, this boundless affection for their vision of the American state of mind ... boogie-woogie-ing their way through rhythm and blues and even rubbing up against the ivory tower where jazzmen hold up and sneer at each other's imperfections and make goo-goo eyes at Schoenberg, Stravinsky and other pedigreed breeds of classical boppers. Keith and Mick were partners in the transmigration of record albums into an erroneous truth about the black man. But it fit the need. The marvellous niggerisation of white kids who were sick to death of the fucking Lindy Hop and Matt Monroe and Pat Boone. Straight ahead with the Stones! Kick out the jams? As simple and hard and primitive as jerking off with the neighbourhood kids. Insistent upon realism – so insistent that it got faded in the wash. Like John David Souther sings: 'I guess I've come a long, long way, but I've changed the words so many times, I lost the melody, and I never even saw it slip away!'

The team of Jagger and Richards created the all-time perfect rock 'n' roll tune: 'I Can't Get No Satisfaction'. The ONLY perfect rock 'n' roll song. Like Michael Lydon told the world: 'The Stones express a unique alienation that is the germ kernel of the rock 'n' roll sensibility – a profound frustration countered by an inchoate yearning for beauty.' He left out the only part about the adolescent capacity for ecstasy. Yearning for that most lofty, evasive ABANDON which has led the saints to slaughter, the sages up the mountains, lovers into their tombs, warriors into horrendous battles, madmen into doom. The Stones touch us where the scab has not yet formed – upon that pinkest, most tender flesh which only becomes calcified when we become ... wise?

DA-DA-DA DAdada DADA: THE MARCH OF TIME

Elvis debuted on RCA with 'Heartbreak Hotel' and it rumbled in the London of 1956.

Fats Domino did eight million with 'Ain't That a Shame', 'Booweevil', etcetera. While Elvis managed to out-sell everybody with eleven million.

1957 was off and running into the cantankerous boobs of the 'sex-bomb' Jayne Mansfield who confirmed how really talented Monroe was. And everybody knew for sure what tits was all about.

Sunday morning and everybody's all dressed up. The nice folks (listening to Sinatra and Boone) have just got up, while the hip folks, they just got home. A film called *Rock Around the Clock* blew away most of the boy scouts.

Mrs Jagger wiped her hands and leaned against the sink. Little Mick was off somewhere, giving Meg a thruppence to feel her up and to try on her dress. 'Though Mick chose the sort of music he's determined to play, he could also have been a very good impersonator,' she said with a proud smile. And Mick dashed through the kitchen on his way to a game of make-believe. 'I can remember him just sitting there,' Mrs Jagger sighed nicely, 'lapping up the hit tunes of the day. Even when he was just a little kiddie.'

CLOSE-UP: the juvenile Jagger, watching the telecast of the annual drag act called the Christmas Pantomime. Trying a few quick sashays and eating a banana. 'He only needed to hear a song a few times,' continued Mrs J., 'and he'd stand up and sing it just exactly like the original. When he was only eleven, he already had the knack.' SLOW DIS-SOLVE.

'And one day,' Keith recalled, 'I met Jagger again, man. Of all places, on the fucking train. I was going to art school and he was going up to the London School of Economics. That must have been about 1960.'[1]

Jagger minces through the hissing doors, a few albums tucked under his arm like an envelope-purse. He rolls his eyes to the ceiling of the train and keeps twisting his ring around his pinky as the engine lurches forward.

'Hi, man,' Keither says, smiling through his bony face.

[1] Robert Greenfield, 'The Rolling Stone Interview: Keith Richard,' *Rolling Stone*, 19 August 1971.

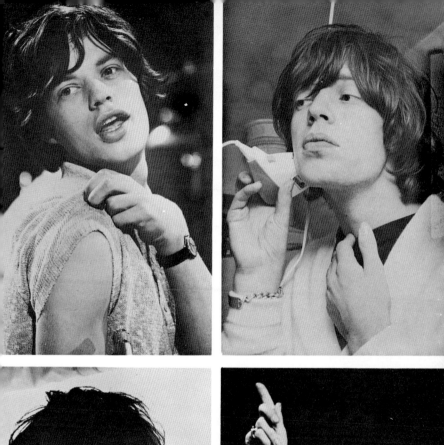

They haven't seen each other for years, but the beat goes on.

'Where ya goin'?' Jagger asks, fondling the albums under his arm: Chuck Berry, Little Walter, Muddy Waters.

'Hey, you into Chuck Berry, man, really?' Keither drools.

'Yeah!' Mick returns proudly. 'I got me a few new albums. Been writin' away to this, ah, Chess Records in Chicago, U.S.A., man, and got me a mailing list thing ... got it together, y'know.'

Keith was a slick dude in those pre-historic days. Going through the English version of the leather trip, during his heavy Teddy boy period, with skin-tights and orange socks. Really rude. Bricks, chains and razor blades. Driving a two-ton through the British museum.

The train is full of these social saboteurs. In their crumby disguises. Nose-pickin', whip-trickin' bombers. Who speak a language which is barely English and who have raised illiteracy to the level of communalism. They are clearly the advance guard, these Teddies, of a class revolt. The bucks from Newcastle storming Windsor!

Meanwhile the deft dandies powder up their Anglo-Saxon variations on themes by Marie Antoinette and intone:

LET THEM EAT ROCK AND ROLL.

But the diversionary tactics do not foil this fierce uprising. Cockney studs rape Lady Windermere at high tea. And the London gentry sees the working class rise gradually in its shops and restaurants like tide water. Staining the fine upholstery of their diction and foot-marking their velvet diplomacy.

Now this new breed plunges through the train doors and enacts its ragged New York choreography, carrying ladies and umbrellaed gentlemen like so much elegant wastepaper in the constant surge of the endless corps de ballet.

Violence is stronger than pedigree. And the London accent merely turns flesh-and-blood flower girls into lame Galateas. So screw Rex Harrison!

Eloquence is a birthright and there is nothing more contemptuous than those who are privileged by something as remote and evasive as birth. Especially when they practice birth control and therefore make membership exclusive.

So the cockney hordes were swelled by the copious contribution of pregnant wenches whose babes prodded like germinating beans from their coarse sacks. Tumbling into the manicured streets, rolling down from the north in smoky autos and motorbikes which rooooar with that industrial brutality which these huge metallic farmers fashion in their hellish grey factories.

Mick Jagger becomes the poet laureate of this tough tidal wave. He ascends like a *perfectly immaculate* Lawrence among the dusty Arabs, without equal in his ability to portray the ennui and desperation of surviving with relative comfort in the long long decline and fall of everything.

It takes magnitude and humanity to articulate the alienation of losers. It is the gift of tears, often the work of derelicts. They construct the intricately simple outcry of the divested: Jews, blacks, Irish, Indians and Chicanos. They plead for those who have gotten nothing in the tide of industry and have gotten the little they owned taken from them. It is an easy lamentation: the blues. But to write a lament for the *winners* who are confronted by the decay of all which they have won, now that is quite another problem. And that was the errand of Mick Jagger. A fragile, twisted saint among the savages. A butterfly in the Bastille. A pawn to the checkered boards of the record industry. Coming up slowly from surf to superstar to suicidologist. Always one perilous step ahead of the holy vestments otherwise called the Emperor's new clothes.

So London rallied to the piping – re-enacting the creative deluge of the Germany of the 1930s – and gradually changed into the ranks of dress-extras who peopled the cast of the most highly overproduced era of full-time slumming which has been staged since the slave rebellion of Spartacus.

Vulgarity became the great social leveller. Violence became the premise for social exchange. A perverse replay of the early American western. Swarming with land-hungry, object-hungry outcasts, drifters and primitives.

When Mick Jagger stepped before his mirror again he was

Oscar Wilde in a leather jacket. The marriage of Alfie and Mary Queen of Scots. The son of professionals with a strong taste for putting on the mongrel, strutting like the common people. Tearing up the King's English with a steam hammer. But in reality, lacking the one most essential plebeian gift, *naïveté*.

A generation of middle-class English kids were absolutely mortified by their refinement. And so they reached out towards the citadel of grossness, America! There in the U.S.A., vulgarity had been raised to the status of a national art.

Jagger had already learned a lot about R and B singing. He was a natural mimic and he had spent hours with his albums from America and the small but deft diet of pop which came regularly over the radio when 'Jazz Club' beamed out its oblique message.

There's no question about the fact that Diddley and Pickett were his major guides through the music of black America. From them he had already learned something about the bull-bottom attack of the great American blues shouters. But then Mick was not a cotton-picking black man with a barbaric wound in his heart. And you can't learn how to bleed from someone else's laceration no matter how hard you try. Still, deep in his heart Jagger desperately wanted to be a Negro. That desire was so intense that if necessary he would *create* a racial fantasy in which his ideal of himself could prevail.

So while Mick, Keith and a few school chums pumped up their musical fictions in various bedrooms of suburban London, Little Richard was at the Oakwood Missionary College of Alabama having thrown over his fabulous career in favour of God; Elvis was taking it easy in the U.S. Army; Lennon and McCartney were jerking off; and Chuck Berry was in jail on a bum rap. Ignorant of each other. Overwhelmed by the enormity of the space between them. Yet they appear to us now as stars in a familiar constellation.

'Ever since then,' David Dalton said, 'Mick and Keith have been conspiring to re-invent the U.S.A., a giant topographical fantasy, hardly less enveloping than Bertolt Brecht and Kurt Weill's imaginary America in the pop-opera *Mahagonny*. It's become such a part of our mental furniture that we recognise it immediately as, at least, a parallel universe. Naïve in the extreme, often exotic as a Japanese western it's still funkier than the one we've got.' And strangely, more realistic.

'To get back to Mick and I,' Keith said, '. . . we found Slim Harpo, and all kinds of people.' But as they got more and more into the professional side of music, they also realised that they couldn't make waves with a little fifty-five-dollar Watkins amp with two guitars plugged in it. They had their eyes on the heavy equipment which started showing up in music store windows as England got the bug.

Now all eyes were on the States. Paris vanished as a world capital and the U.S.A., a nation which had always seemed obvious and crass and materialistic, became the mecca of kids. Anything American was beautiful: hamburgers, packaged cookies and Lipton's flow-thru teabags. Beautiful! There were no movies like American movies. America even had the edge on chicks and dudes. Brando and Dean. Gangsters and Indians. Marilyn and Mansfield. And with the movies and the imported TV series came slang – the portal to black culture. While in things chic, even Pierre Cardin agreed that the most inventive contemporary fashions were Levis and T-shirts. And of course, there was the MUSIC. Beautiful!

Mixed with the exoticism of black culture was the fantasised image of Indian America: reflected everywhere in a wondrous new *Kipling, U.S.A.* Kokomo, Natchez, Mississippi, Wichita! What a blast! When stripped of their ancient agony, the black man and the Indian became the perfect mannequins of the new American fashion. The hyperbolic view from over the Atlantic.

Chuck Berry, the Baudelaire of southern fantasy, had replaced the overwhelming gloom of Mississippi, Georgia and Alabama with an endless saga of troubadour illusions which he dispensed like a rural medicine man. The infection of his trouble-free daydream crossed the Atlantic. It also was the basis for the creative folklore of such cosmopolitan swampers as Creedence's John Fogarty who never saw the Okefenokee but drank up all that local colour on phonograph records when he was a kid back in Oakland, California.

Meanwhile strange Brian Jones, suave, cruel, educated, a jazz aficionado and future Rolling Stone, meandered his way through Scandinavia, playing a little harmonica at cafés, getting some coin or a meal, and giving the northern lights the once-over.

And 1961 was slowly turning into 1962, with a little help from some millionaires. Elvis posed with his Rolls in front of his colonial mansion in Grassland, Tennessee. Jayne Mansfield posed with muscleman Mickey Hargitay in her heart-shaped swimming pool in Beverly Hills, California. The Blue Diamonds did one hundred thousand dollars with 'Ramona', and the Ventures broke into Europe with 'Walk, Don't Run'. Meanwhile a bunch of clean-cut novices called the Shadows were turning a number of novel instrumental tricks in England, constructing that high wall of popularity which the Beatles would soon hurdle in order to become the new, first-place English group.

1962 opened with the incredible Mr. Ray Charles laying on 'Hit the Road Jack'. Edith Piaf was the reigning queen of song in the world of otherwise dubious French pop. And in America at the Graumann's Chinese Theatre on Hollywood Boulevard, the film *West Side Story* (with its Bernsteinian quasi-'jazz&pap') premièred and became a major force in the reappraisal of pop as *art*. Suggesting to the mass audience of cinema something already suggested some fifteen years earlier on Broadway by Agnes DeMille in *Oklahoma* and *Carousel*: that popular musical entertainment could be serious at least to the extent that it made a departure from Hallmark lyrics and endings, that dance (the most *American* art, along with jazz, of all the arts) could propel a dramatic impulse as an expressive form rather than simply decorating a scene or two with tap-dancing, high-kicking girlie-gams. Move Over Beethoven! The Lindy and the Waltz are doomed. Crooners

37

and Swooners are finished. Apollo's truckin' with ole Dionysus at the Paladium. And Enter the White Englishman as Nigger ... Doin' a Slow Drag!

It was 1962 and despite the strong example of Bill Haley and the Comets, the group idea was not yet popular in English music. The charts were filled with straight jazz from people like Acker Bilk, the souped-up electrodes of the Tornados and their multi-million $eller 'Telstar', along with Cliff Richard, Brenda Lee, and other strictly solo performers.

MEDIUM SHOT: Mick, Keith and Dick Taylor look in awe at the passing parade. In the BG, MUSIC UP & OUT – a trad band is playing, the lemonade of dance hall pop music.

MICK: (with Andy Hardy grimace, CLOSE-UP) When we make it, maties (Gulp) we'll be in the money. We'll be lolling about in limousines and we'll be cruising around the world in luxury whenever we feel like it.

KEITH: (a wise nod, CLOSE-UP) You know you're talking rubbish. (Bogart frown) I know you're talking rubbish. But let's keep the gag goin' ... just to give us something to think about.

MICK: (with a smile, CLOSE-UP) Yeah.

KEITH: (again the wise nod, CLOSE-UP) But let's get this whole bit straight. No matter what we do we'll never be up there in the Hit Parade. That's impossible with this sort of music. We're a fuckin' minority. . . there aren't many fans who'll ever understand all this way-out blues stuff. It's Elvis or Cliff . . . that's what they want. But if we have a real go at it, really work our material, well . . . we could get a bit of work and we could build up a little following by persuading people to like the same things we like.

MICK: (nodding B-movie-style and clearing his throat, MEDIUM SHOT of the two boys, sitting at a table at the Bricklayers' Arms) You're probably right Keith. But I'd like to give it a go. (Gulp) Wanna come in with me ... really chance our luck? (Andy Hardy and Judy Garland

38

take one last, noisy suck on their ice-cream sodas and get up, smiling. They shake hands and exit left as we PAN to the calendar reading 'FEBRUARY, 1962.' SLOW FADE OUT.)

LOLLING ABOUT THE BRICKLAYERS' ARMS OR VICTORY AT TEA

A public house in London's Soho district. Through the swinging brown door with its cut-glass and frosted window comes an occasional tart. Pre-Pygmalion dollies, vending their wilted flower to street-traders who speak a language which is not quite English. An old fella with a black and white checked cap sits in the corner near the stove tooth-lessly munching a sandwich and downing a pint of bitters. Over there, by the window, Mr and Mrs Muff dawdle in their perpetually sauced and slow-motion argument. Taking time out occasionally to order another pair. Then returning to their unheated debate as to whether it was 1932 or 1933 that the electric went out in County Wicklow, Ireland. Mr Peter Finch Tate has got holes in both elbows of his sweater and ole Mrs Hurphy is crying again 'cause it's the tenth anniversary of the death of her English terrier, Maude.

It's not a fancy pub, the Bricklayers' Arms, but it's got a genial atmosphere, and a body can let his mouth go without regretting it the next morning. The keep is a nice sort who will run a tab if you're a little short towards the end of the month.

He's a large man, the barman, with a lot of red in his cheeks. A beard and a moustache circling his smile. 'Sure, I remember them fellas very well indeed. There was two of them all the time, y'know. Without a bob, just laying about, they were. The one with the mouth, y'know, and the other one, the skinny one. And sometimes another youngster or two also, their mates, y'know. Pale lads they were, with *all* that hair.'

He let them run a slate because they seemed like good

39

sorts. 'But strange talkers, they were. I mean they'd talk 'bout all kinds of musical subjects. They talked a streak 'bout this music of theirs. Whereas, y'see, most of me customers, now, they like to talk over a good trotter or maybe a soccer match.'

The chippies sometimes hung about with the boys for a few minutes, getting off on their crazy slang and bawdy humour. Feeding them the bottom of a beer or a fag or two. 'Mick was such a fine, elegant sort, y'know,' one of the retired whores reports with a deep red smile. 'He was always very proper to a lady and never spoke out-a-turn, while the other one, y'know, the skinny lad with the crazy eyes, now he was never above feelin' a little for free. I mean, it ain't proper in a public place to be laying hands on a lady.'

The Bricklayers' Arms is gone, transformed into a whole-sale business, but there's a plaque on the wall which remembers the nights when the Rolling Stones laid their battle plans for up-turning the world of music.

Brian Jones, back in England after roaming pointlessly, dropped by the Bricklayer's Arms occasionally. It was there that he had his first conversation with Mick and Keith. They talked R and B and jazz, two opposing forces which seemed as if they could never merge. The one, jazz, intellectual, the only popular musical alternative in those days for people who didn't want to listen to Bach full-time but couldn't get into the adolescent incantations of Elvis. The other, rhythm and blues, pre-intellectual, volatile and funky long before the advent of Funk.

Keith and Brian were drifting. Essentially they didn't give a shit. Mick was keeping his lifeboats on board even if it crowded his style a little. He kept plugging away at the School of Economics.

LAST MINUTE FLASHES

The Yankees were in last place. There was a newspaper strike in New York City during Xmas of 1962. A good-natured kid in Dallas destroyed a dream. In the Arctic, the Russians were popping nuclear toys. The Queen's annual message was flashed to the hungry millions via Telstar, and on December 26th, the team of Jagger, Richards, Taylor and a sometime-piano player named Ian Stewart had a full-scale disaster at their début booking at the Piccadilly Club.

........................*click* ... *click Alexis? Are you still there?*

Yes ... *I'm here. It's just a very bad connection.*

Right ... *tell me something, it was about this time that you first met Mick Jagger, isn't that right?*

Yes, that's right. I'm not very good on dates, y'know, but it was just about the end of 1962 or perhaps the very beginning of 1963.

Rita has on his big coat, the fur number, despite the fact that the Fourth of July is over and he's the temperature of a medium-rare fillet. But a grand entrance requires a bit of suffering, and so he endures the sixteen minutes required to make a medium-splash in the very small pond known as Max's Kansas City.

HaaaaaateeeeeeeeHeeeeeeee ... Bang! ... Crash! ... Blah ... Blah ... Blah ... Blah ... farout! Sthere's-Andy-noooooow. . . gracious . . . wwwhat-a-biiiitch, my-deeear ... sooopastaaaar! FAB-U-LOUS! ...FAB-U-LOUS! ... dannydannydannydannydanny-lillianlillianlillianbiiiiiitch! Kitschbitch, my-deeear, kittschbitch!

There's a score of harebrained children ... *they are locked in the nursery* ... *they got earphone heads* ... *they got dirty necks* ... *they're so twentieth century.* Half a dozen ribbon clerks in revolutionary drag are assembled at the door. They do such a good job of ignoring you that you can't get through. 'Excuse me, muther.' Sentinels of the nouveau-hip. *Despair All Ye Who Enter Here*, a dainty Dante whispers to a large blond woman with the face of a battlefield.

The Bar: infinity on the rocks. 'I've done nothing but talk about myself all evening. My god, but I'm sorry. Let's talk

41

about you for a while ... what did *you* think of my last album?'

'Excuse me.'

The terribly smart types standing five-deep at the bar in their fifteen-dollar pre-worn Levis and Bonwit-shit gaze steadfastly through outrageous Rita who retaliates for their flashy indifference by dropping the big fur over her shoulders and clearing a six-foot space as she models it with lots of elbow. 'Hot stuff, folks,' she sings, 'excuse your muther, my dear, but she's not well tonight.'

The typists give Rita the New Jersey *ain't that jist aaaaaweful numbba*, while their wide-tied steeds manfully mumble gymnasium commentaries and other locker room axioms. Meanwhile, everybody takes notes so they can do Rita justice back at the office on Monday morning.

The Front Dining Room: the banks of the River Styx where the unworthy must wait five hundred years. A pissy purgatorio where the foot of the fabled stairway to heaven has its guarded entrance. Six Novenas and thirty-seven steps upward to the realm of the muses and an occasional concert by Alice Cooper – that vaudevillian Jagger with runs in his stockings – or the Velvets in their most recent reincarnation.

But Rita is one of the Chosen People who inherited the Promised Land when the Beautiful People lost their lease on life. So he chitchats his way in a straight line directly to the great nave itself. The Inner-Sanctum and Grande Chambre of the Great Oz in the heart of downtown Emerald City.

Thunder! Lightning! Shooting Flames! 'It isn't Kansas anymore, is it Toto.' It's the backroom at Max's Kansas City, and there among the tables and chairs and tenderised sirloins sits the hysterically casual cast of characters, hanging out till closing for fear of what will be said about them if they leave. Lolling over an African lobster. Stirring reds into the gerabonza beans. Recounting the *maaaaavelus* tales of torment of an East Side bummer. Declaring the liberation of Ann Miller. Revolt into *schtick*. The price of grass. The effect of wearing high heels on natural birth according to *Rolling Stone*. The steady decanonisation of saints; and the antemortem of things postmortem. The announcement of the excommunication of impurists, infidels and heretics by the great tribunal which sits nightly at the big circular table in the corner. Ensconced behind invisible screens, working the levers which make the thunder and the lightning and the shooting flames. Oz Incarnate – with a white wig and sunglasses. Keeping his misties to himself. The Clown as Ringmaster. A Woolworth Diaghilev.

And Rita laughs his enormous, boisterous laugh, with all those rancid teeth flashing green and black. 'If he ever took off those sunglasses,' Rita roars uncontrollably, 'they'd find out that he's not circumcised!' She *loves* it and keeps laughing, gradually becoming hysterical, as she pulls off the fur and fans himself with a menu. 'My dear, I could die I'm so fuckin' on tonight! . . . what do you mean: HOT? *How rude!* . . . personally, I think it's the coldest July we've had in yearsssss.' And he pulls his coat back over his shoulders and shivers for everybody.

Jackie Curtis pays his respects. Cool, incandescent, brilliant and cunting. A fantastic brain alive behind the glittered eyes. He kisses Rita on the forehead, maternally — the mama of *Juliet of the Spirits*. For him the Great Oz dropped his screens a long time ago, so Jackie is not afraid of the little man, and takes his leave. *Good night, sweet prince*.

Rita in answer to the adjoining queen: 'Paco? . . . I haven't seen his box in eight days. How *very* kind and thoughtful of you to ask, you vicious cocksucker! Now move your arse and don't bug me again or I'll rearrange your fuckin' eyelashes for you!' Exit queen *à la allegro*. 'Some fairies have no class,' Rita concludes seriously. 'She calls me sister in the john to get a toke on a joint and then she tries to fuck with my head 'cause she gets a little stoned. Some sister! If that's gay liberation, my dear, I'm better off out in the street with male impersonators from Jersey. But that isn't what I want to talk to you about. . . . What I'm interested in tonight, Fred, is this matter of the party. . . what do you mean, *what party?* You know fuckin' well that I mean *the* party. Yes, *that* one. The Stones Party! . . . I'm not interested in the politics,

Fred my man. All I know is that you're a big shit with the folks at Atlantic. I mean with all your connections, Fred-la, certainly you can get me one *little* invite. I mean, *really*, what's such a big deal anyways. . . so what, *only five hundred guests* . . . who belongs there more than me? Now I ask you, if you really want the giants of rock music and the giants of hip society, my dear, you know who has to be there, now don't you.' And he does a little number with the fur coat. 'I mean, far be it for me to tell you about the 499 – but, honey, if you're not looking into the gorgeous eyes of number 500, well, sweetheart, you're just stone mad, that's all. What do you mean: *Maybe?* . . . now look, look, I've never been the kind to push. Now you know that, but, Fred my dear, either I get an invitation to that goddamn party or heads will roll. I mean *heads*. I am so fucking tired of being the token faggot at your half-ass little press parties for pre-pubescent rock 'n' roll brats. I am so fuckin' tired of all these goddamn closet types shouting power to the people while they treat me like shit. I'm so bored to death with you and your hetero-sexual friends . . . the little sonofabitch at *Rolling Stone* who got married so nobody would guess that the reason he swishes his ass all over the place is simply because he's a fucking cocksucker just like everybody else in the world. And the big assistant to the assistant dangling his wife and kids in front of everybody when he isn't getting fucked silly at some leather-gangbang. I'm so tired of all this shit with all you liberated phony sonsofbitches-and-bastards and your fuckin' supremacy routine. *So get me an invitation, Fred, y'hear!* Otherwise, honey, Atlantic will be sending you a tulle formal as your Christmas bonus next year.'

Mick was still high from the second show in Seattle when he boarded the touring plane, *The Tongue*, en route to San Francisco. 'Used to be able to do that with one han' before me strength-to-weight ratio changed,' Mick says as he chins himself on the luggage rack and then hangs upside down and lets the blood rush to his large lips.

As the stewardess finishes her lecture on the use of the life jackets and oxygen masks, Mick settles back into his seat and fastens up, peering momentarily out the window and saying with an unusual touch of doom: 'This is the most critical part right here. The power turn. Y'know, if it's gonna happen . . .' He half-smiles, bites down on his lip, closes his eyes and puts his head back against the seat.

Even before take-off the champagne and orange juice makes its morning rounds. There's also a buffet of raw vegetables, crackers and heaps of yoghurt in the galley for the ones with the nerve to ingest solids at this hour. Bobby Keys is muttering: 'Ah cum back ta mah rum laaast nite ta git sum sleep and therez uh gayng-baaang goin' on der. In mah own bed. Chick luked like Joe Palooka.'

Mick: 'Luke what?'

Bobby: 'Lahk a bus mechanic.' Mick's eyes get that ole glint and he flashes the Jagger smile. Everybody knows what he's thinking, but somehow nobody ever jokes about it.

Now nothing but the teeming boredom of mid-air entrapment, minimised by the removal of lots of the seats so there's room to layabout or pace or get a game of chance going. . . but confinement all the same. And the contagious electronic song of this great metallic bird, sailing over the American landscape. Northern forests, strips of coastline, snowy peaks, wide valleys and the monstrous geometry of farmlands: an airborne and verdant Mondrian. Then slowly in the south a light begins to gleam over the horizon, just vaguely at first, but constantly growing. A strange music can be heard in the distance. Unhuman . . . perhaps divine. The hills appear to swell and move, turning first black and then purple. A cloud shaped like a guitar floats by slowly while gigantic papier-mâché groupies descend and wrap their luscious legs around the fuselage of the aircraft and slowly pump their marvellous thighs against the metallic siding, making a sound like dozens of chicks walking in rain-filled galoshes. The sky opens up and turns golden as a shower of acid, Mesc and DMT makes its spectacular display. The distant music grows louder and the dazzling shower of light swells suddenly. Tom Paine and Geronimo stride across the

45

sky and blow their trumpets with silvered lips, while Jesus, Buddha and Sarah Bernhardt shake out the mantle of the bay and spread it like a cloth beneath the looming craft called *Tongue*. And is it really God who now speaks to us, rising steadily like a white tornado from the land of the sky-blue water? *Also Sprach Zarathurstra!!!!* . . . The theme from *2001*! No, its Bill Graham casting a shadow from coast to coast and speaking thus: 'Look Upon My Works, Ye Mighty, and Despair!'

When the mist settles, we see SAN FRANCISCO. Cradle of Western Civilisation! *God, ain't life just like a movie!*

PAS DE TROIS

From the window, through the iron gate, the light was cut like cookies into diamond-shapes. Yellow light . . . electric moonlight coming through the faded shade of the apartment across the way. The sound too, of a phonograph came from up above, mixed with our radio. *You take your choice at this time, the brave old world or the slide to the depths of decline* . . . Mick is singing to us from overhead, accompanied by the random thumping of their feet, and the vague exchange of air coming through the wall where someone sleeps next door. I too sleep, or almost . . . conscious enough to take the joint from whatever fingers offer it. While someone laughs outside, and Alyson sells us something between the cuts. And then plays another Genya Ravan tune.

His hand comes down upon my leg and she props herself up high enough to look into my face and say: 'Are you two really brothers?'

'No, we only say that 'cause it gets us off to think about it,' I reply.

'Well,' she smiles, burying her nose under my arm and talking though the sheets, 'you look like brothers. You act like brothers. And you even smell like brothers.'

Ah, tall clean, lean and deeply tanned . . . crazy lady. What a dream. Rotating slowly so that the diamond-shapes make a perfect bodice around her breasts. Her burnished honey hair spread like a sprinkler on a summer-lawn across my chest. Her leg thrown over his belly and her fingers working ever so delicately upon his immaculate chest ... while she ponders the mixture of smoke in the yellow air above us.

'San Francisco,' Mick said slowly, perhaps a bit guarded since he knows the power of the myth he is confronting, '. . . San Francisco was . . . well, we've always had strange times there. Politics . . . like that. I don't believe the intensity.'

A toilet flushes. Somebody across the way is pacing in the yellow light, sending a shadow into our bed where it rolls softly over us. 'Your brother ... he never talks?' she murmurs.

'Not very much.'

'What's his name?'

'Ask him.'

As she begins to pose the question, he puts his mouth over her lips. The people upstairs are having an argument ... their voices coming through the music in short, frosty gusts. Making us retreat into each other, coiling limb upon limb until we are a single cell propelled by a single energy.

A schizophrenic geography. Bodies not intended for each other. Their very proximity is a crime against nature. Oakland: broad-shouldered, mute, and heavy into bravado. Berkeley: intellectual, opinionated and obsessed with the transformation of ideals into actions. And long, lean, clean, San Francisco: as self-conscious and old fashioned as Paris. Living on the memory of years of aristocratic pretentions followed by a single fleeting summer of reality . . . the corpses of rebels who were so vital that they had to escape from this city in order to have their rebellion. A place which loves education and loathes intellectuals. Admires the Arts but detests artists. Gives birth to a new music but disowns it in preference for a second-hand symphony orchestra and a fancy-dress ball pretending to be an opera season. A city which outlaws graffiti but plasters every available opera house seat-back,

marble slap and museum façade with the names not of great
artists but of petty money donors. Proud, haughty, middle-
class and convinced that every time a stone falls into the
Pacific it's written up in *The New York Times*.

Mick looks at the lights from across the bay in Oakland
where, at the Coliseum, guitars blew for the first show and
vibes never got up for the second. The audience kept the
enthusiasm at a minimum by filtering the music through
their consciousness of rock as capitalist diversion. Entertainment with a contraceptive.

Everybody is watching out for rip-offs!

Fraud!

Hype!

Inequity!

Profit!

The militants are searching lyrics for social conscience,
while heads loll in a euphoria which precludes the reality
of sound. 'I think you know we're with you on Vietnam and
everything,' Mick says a bit sheepishly to the assembled
press before the concert. 'It's just that I don't find it a thing to
sing songs about. It's music for us, and supposed to be fun. We
want you to get up and dance, y'know, and not sit back and
be worried about what you're *supposed* to do.'

Backstage in the dressing room of the grey Coliseum,
there's a poster of Bill Graham giving the world the finger.
It hangs over a table where Graham has provided a buffet of
beer and cheeses and hard rolls. The food has been flung all
over the place. The poster is smeared with blue cheese.
Graham reacts to the financial strategy of these colossal
superstars with a perfect Grahamcracker: 'Mick Jagger
may be a great performer, but he's an egotistical creep as a
person.'

A dozen months later, Billy's presenting Mick and the
boys at Winterland. Four incredibly well-organised concerts
with the definitive Graham touch. And a couple of bashes at
the Trident in Sausalito and at a mincing burgundy-and-
gold-leaf French restaurant in San Francisco where the grand
impresario of rock is all blown up with pride and good

48

fellowship. The Graham enigma artlessly combines energy, machismo and love into a persistent metaphor: 'When you think of this moment . . . be very careful.' He is unquestionably the singularly most interesting figure in the business: marvellously lovable and absolutely hateful. Devoted to freedom of expression for *everyone* but his enemies. He barred the major music press from his theatres very early in the game. Emphatically a peacenik who threatens physical violence if he is offended. And he is easily offended. Capable – with a grin – of every possible hype but also one of the first to rage about rip-offs and con-jobs. Devoted to the concept that the music belongs to the people . . . at whatever ticket price the traffic will bear. Yet one of the most generous men alive and the *one* promoter in rock 'n' roll who gives a shit about artists, their comfort *and* their art. El Graham, standing like a bull-dog at the side door of Winterland, San Francisco, before the second Stones' show, shouting to no one in particular: 'Move! Who do you think you are, Johnny Superstar! Use the front door! Do you understand English! *Front Door! Front Door*, ass-hole, like everyone else!' And then he smiles a big, profoundly good smile.

Meanwhile someone has called the fire department, muttering something diabolical about Winterland being on fire. Five or six engines, police cars, ambulances and sundry hook-and-ladder jobs come screaming to the rescue with whirling red-green lights and supernatural beings in rubber-suits. A spectre in the stony night which sent scores of hallucinogenic-freaks into colossal bummers.

Mick takes a swig from the bottle while the show's medicine man checks his heart rate: 'Like, well . . . California doesn't really have anything to do with the rest of America, now does it?'

'Do you drink like that all the time?' she asked him, wiping the booze from his chin. But he doesn't answer. He sits up and stares directly into the yellow light coming through the window. . . . *living a life of constant change, every day means a turn of a page . . . Yesterday's papers are such bad news . . . the same thing applies to me and you.* Mick serenading us in a little voice, confined inside a four-transistor portable sitting on the nightstand.

'What's with your brother?' she asks, getting a little pissed by his silence.

'He's bored,' I mutter.

'With me?' she huffs.

'With you, with me, with everything. Some people get sleepy after they come. He gets bored.'

'I get hungry,' she says.

'Yeah?' I say flatly.

'Yeah ...' she says.

I was like any other kid, Mick said, which is why all the rest identified with me. I was just the same as they were, except that I'd jumped the tracks a bit more, that's all. All the stuff about my leading them and perverting them or whatever, it's ... we just sort of went along together, didn't we?

The first Bay Area junket, in the Coliseum in Oakland, was a suburban quickie: a bit o'whoring in the countryside. Altamont was a cosmic defecation. The Winterland gig was a live sex show, a simulated hand-job for the masses. A *ménage à trois* in music: from the hall of the mountain king to the intensive care ward at Camrillo. From acid and arcana to Ripple and resignation. ... *What a shame they always want to start a fight.*

'... seems like I get drunk most nights now. ... I don't really know why,' she says quietly, putting her head on his chest and staring at the ceiling.

'He's driving us to drink ... Nixon is ... it all started with that big famine when he closed up the Mexican border ... remember? ... Grass was going for forty-five dollars and up ... man, what a pisser that was.'

'... I really don't like it, y'know ... booze, I mean. It's

not good for you, y'know. And I feel terrible the next day
. . . just terrible.'

'Mick drinks quite a lot, doesn't he?'

'Well,' she says slowly, rolling her head slowly back and
forth on his chest and, with arms stretched upward, playing
an imaginary piano with her long fingers, '. . . y'know how it
is with the English. They never really got into dope the way
we did over here. I mean, they always had a sort of happy-
home-life scene going, if you know what I mean. Like England, y'know has never gotten wise to the fact that the whole
fuckin' world is falling apart. The Empire . . . and all that
shit, y'know. They're still into God, King and Country.'

'Somebody told me . . . who the fuck told me that? . . .
anyway, somebody told me that the hippies appeared briefly
in Hyde Park in the summer of 1968, until the first frost.
Then they went home to their mums and dads.'

She laughs. So does my brother.

'Anyway,' she murmurs, '. . . Mick drinks. Once, y'know,
at a party here in New York . . . he got sort of gassed.'

'Yeah?'

She curls up with a pillow and laughs.

'What's that all about?' I ask, but she keeps lolling with a
recollection – ignoring me – and smiling with what looks like
a bit of blush.

He gets up and walks to the window, stretching his lean
limbs like a dancer, crouching down and bouncing and
twisting his torso. She watches him with cool, frosted eyes:
digging the bod.

'You ever make it with Mick?' I ask.

'No,' he says.

'No,' she says.

Then they look at each other and laugh.

'I thought you were talking to me,' she giggles.

'There's this very famous dancer . . .' he starts, but then
reconsiders and goes silent.

'What about it?' she prompts.

He goes into the head and stands wide-legged at the john,
his ass going muscular. 'Forget it,' he says over the cascade.

'. . . once,' she whispers to me, '. . . once he got very drunk No, not really drunk. But he had a few drinks, and . . .' suddenly she is ten years younger '. . . y'know, like, he felt me up a couple of times.'

'Yeah? . . . Mick did that?'

She laughs. And then, after a moment, she frowns. 'But that's as far as it went.'

For two years I had been thinking with every guy, 'He's great, but he's not Mick Jagger.' And then with Mick, all I could think was, he's great, but he's not Mick Jagger. He has to work at being Mick Jagger, you know? Some mornings he wakes up and says, 'I feel so fragile this morning . . . be gentle,' and I think: 'This is the Mick I idolised?'

She watches him as he pulls on his shorts, arranges and rearranges his basket in front of the mirror, turning his head to the side and finally pressing his lips together and nodding with some strange approval.

'The thing is,' Mick said, 'it's very easy for people to believe that's what I'm like,' and then he said after a thoughtful pause: '. . . I don't understand the connection between music and violence. I just know that I get very aroused by music, but it doesn't arouse me violently. I never went to a rock-and-roll show and wanted to smash the windows or beat anybody up afterwards. I feel more sexual than actually physically violent. I get a sexual feeling and I want to fuck as soon as I've been playing. I cool down very quickly. I can come off the stage and be back to normal in five minutes.'

. . . I remember you in Hemlock Road in nineteen fifty-six, you were a faggy little leather boy with a smaller piece of stick.

'Sonabitch!' someone shouts upstairs. And there's this huge crash on the ceiling.

The guy next door is startled from his sleep and cries out in momentary terror. Across the way, someone puts out the yellow light and the diamond-pattern vanishes from our room. He kisses her just once, very gently, their lips hardly touching. Then he rolls over on his side, snorting, and wraps his legs around mine. She tucks her head under my chin and snuggles up with her tits against my side. The transistor is selling something . . . *tellin' me more and more about some useless*

52

information, supposed to fire my imagination. I reach out towards
the sound in the darkness and silence it.

We lay there in the dark.

Then he picks up the end of a sentence and speaks as if
everybody's been waiting for him to finish what he started to
say a half hour ago. . . .

'. . . and this dancer, well, like he said he didn't want
to make it with him cause he's too skinny, y'know. Fuckin'
fool!'

*Well, I am just a monkey man, I'm glad you are a monkey woman,
too.*

BLUES SOLO FOR ALEXIS

(*Moderate Blues Beat*)

'The first influence of blues in England, as best I recall,' Alexis pondered, 'was the impact of the coloured G.I.s, y'know, who came over during the war and also the phonograph records which they carted around with them. That gave us our first taste, really, of blues. I know, for instance, that there was one bloke by the name of Eric Lister singing blues and working with sorta early blues players up in Manchester at the end of the 1940s or so. Which was the same time as the Chris Barber band, the first blues band that I was in. That ... oh, let's see, that was in 1948. Now we ourselves were strictly involved in the folk side of the blues. But, I suppose, really, that the basis of it was carried along mainly by the skiffle movement.'

[1] Greenfield.

WITH TWO-PART HARMONY ON THE CHORUSES

(*Rocking Beat; Not Too Fast*)

'*Ealing Jazz Club*' (*Flashing Neon Sign*), *at the end of the Central Underground Line*. 'Alexis Korner really got this scene together,' Keith announced. 'He's been playin' in jazz clubs for ages and he knew all the connections for gigs. So we went up there. The first or the second time Mick and I were sittin' there, Alexis Korner gets up and says, "We got a guest to play some guitar. He's come from Cheltenham. All the way up from Cheltenham just to play for ya." Suddenly it's *Elmore James*, this cat, man, doin' it. And it's Brian, man, he's sittin' on his little ... he's bent over ... da-da-da, da-da-da ... I said, what? What the fuck? Playin' bar slide guitar!'[1] *Holy Shit!*

Charlie Watts: '*That's the guv-nor. If anyone is going to get rhythm and blues away in this country, that's the boy. There's nobody more dedicated than he is. Honest, it's a pleasure to work with him. . . .*'[2]

Alexis: Chris Barber and Ken Colyer were the leaders of the skiffle movement. I was with the very first Barber-Colyer Skiffle Band, and when they split up, I left because I didn't actually enjoy skiffle. It was all right, but, to tell the truth, it was not much more than good-time music. And I had some ideas of my own about what music should communicate to an audience.

Keith: '*Most of the clubs at the time were filled with dixieland bands, traditional jazz bands. An alternative to all that Bobby Vee stuff. There was a big boom in that: the stomp, stompin' about, weird dancing, just tryin' to break the ceiling to a two-beat. That was a big scene. That's where Alexis made the breakthrough. He managed to open it up at the Ealing Club. Then he moved on to the Marquee and R and B started to become the thing. And all these traddies, as they were called, started getting worried. So they started this bitter opposition.*'[3]

Alexis: There is no exact American counterpart to skiffle. In England, I'll tell you where we got it from. We've always understood that skiffles were really the same as South Side Rent Parties. A Skiffle Party in which, oh, a couple of people would play mainly straight blues all night long . . . while people drank and messed around generally. Sixty cents a head to come in, y'know, and have a merry ole time, and that way you raised your rent. Which was quite an accomplishment for blokes like Mick and the boys. They were pretty poor if they were living the student life and didn't want to stay on at home where they could at least get bed and board.

Lennon's first gigs were with a skiffle band.

[2] Rolling Stones, as told to Pete Goodman, *Our Own Story* (New York: Bantam Books, 1965).
[3] Greenfield.

Ya don't say. Now that's somethun, ain't it.

Aw, shut up, Paul, and go home, will ya.

Alexis (aside): People are being unfair if they look back on skiffle too frivolously. Every musical movement that is big enough to be a popular movement has got to produce some good musicians who wouldn't have had the incentive to start playing without it.

As far as we were concerned, that's what skiffle was. And the reason that I split off from it was because it got to the point where it was half-way country and western rather than being, at least as I saw it then, a proper Negro music. We were very wrapped up in the idea of the music of the American Negro. It didn't occur to us that it was not the kind of music which white musicians should play – that was always an American preoccupation, since, at least to us, music was music and it was valid no matter who performed it if it was performed properly. I split away from skiffle because it was no longer blues. Skiffle, at least in my head, was always piano and guitar, more or less, because they were the instruments you were most likely to find laying about in somebody's apartment, y'know. Washboard was also fair enough, if you wanted that sort of sound ... you know ... how should I say ... more or less a primitive sort of Chicago sound.

Promoters got turned on by the success of the skiffle movement and that encouraged them to book American blues acts which had never gotten much play outside of a small American clique. The first ones to be brought over to England were the great folkies like Leadbelly and Big Bill Broonzy. Later the Chicago blues stars also got gigs: Muddy Waters, Howlin' Wolf and Sonny Boy Williamson.

At this point I decided that I really didn't like any of the sounds around at the time. And I met up with someone who was really a blues buff ... uh ... who played harmonica, twelve-string guitar and various things ... and we just both liked the same sort of people and liked to play the same way. His name was Cyril Davies. Actually at the time he was working at a very successful skiffle club in town, and I used

56

to go up and guest there occasionally ... but when I sat in, I just played straight blues.

Charlie Watts: 'Alexis and Cyril deserved all the success going and it was a tragedy when Cyril suddenly died.

(Slow drum roll ... New Orleans style ... all the dudes in black tails and top hats with black fabric hanging from the big bass drums ... slow march for Cyril ... When the Saints Come Marchin' In.)

Charlie: That original band really moved. It was great playing with them ... with guys like Andy Webb and Jack Bruce. And it was all free and easy. We had this scene going for us at the Ealing and at the Marquee and it was all so fuckin' impromptu y'know, that blokes like Mick could just get up and sing with us if they felt like it. That's how Keith and Brian came to sit in too.' [1]

Alexis: And Cyril said to me one day: 'Look, what about ... ah ... if we close this club down, would you open it up again with me as a blues club?'

So I said: 'Yes, OK.'

Ah, I don't know exactly when that was, but it must have been about 1954. It was called The Roundhouse, a club situated over a pub, on the second floor. Not *the* Roundhouse, but a different one on the corner of Wardour Street and Brewer Street. That was the first regularly going blues club in London. The focus for lots of young people like Mick – really a tiny group of kids who were very excited about American blues. It was essentially Davies and me, and odd people would now and then drop in and guest with us. John Baldry would come by 'cause y'know he was into it back then – one of the first English blues singers he was.

And then we wanted to go electric and the club was too small for the sound. 1958 or thereabouts. But it was no revolution ... I mean nothing like the Dylan situation when we went electric. After all, I was playing amplified guitar back

[1] Rolling Stones.

in 1947. Many American jazz guitarists used a bit of amplification in those days. But nothing very powerful, y'know.

However, we found that none of the traditional jazz clubs in which we used to play occasionally would accept us ... because we were playing electric and they wouldn't put up with it. So we had to open our own club finally in 1962, just to be able to play the music we liked. It was St Patrick's Day and we opened a brand new club called the Ealing Jazz Club. And it was very strange, y'know. We put up maybe a dozen posters locally, and we thought maybe we'd get a little group on the first night. By the second Saturday it was completely packed, with people coming down from Scotland. It was simply a matter of being the right band at the right place at the right time.

You got the feeling in those days that something had to change because the music in England was very stagnant at the time. And somehow it seemed to many of us that *this* blues band was what was going to change it. It's something ... a feeling, y'know ... which you can't really repeat ten years later. But the music we were playing just *felt* very, very much more alive than anything else that was going on. It felt right.

It had gotten to the point with the trad bands where you knew exactly what and where the trumpet and clarinet were going to play. Not that you can't also tell that with blues, but blues is *so* basic, y'know, that you have to do extra musical things with it that even you as the performer don't know about till they happened.

The trad musicians got used to playing their best solos. Now as I see it, in blues it's very important to recreate a *mood*, and you're inclined to use exactly the same musical devices each time to produce this mood successfully at each performance. In jazz that's not a valid approach because jazz is essentially an improvised music ... within a framework, of course. And, in jazz, if the improvisation isn't strong enough, then the music simply isn't worth hearing. To endlessly repeat your solos defeats the purpose ... and that's what had happened to the trad jazz bands by 1962.

58

*Bunch of mean-ass teen-agers on the steps of the ballroom, jeering.
The Doorman, getting pushy, says: 'You're nothin' but bums and
beatniks, that's all y'are. You're gonna end up on skid row, y'are.
So get your arse along or we'll tan it for ya.'*

Alexis: I started doing gigs at the Marquee Jazz Club during
the 1950s at some point. Just occasional gigs with Chris Barber. Chris and I have always kept a kinda funny contact,
and two or three years before I had formed Blues Incorporated as a full-time working band, Cyril and I used to
back up Chris's wife when she did her fifteen or twenty
minute blues set. So we had worked the Marquee back even
before we had Blues Incorporated going.

The Marquee served an excellent purpose in the growth of
blues and rhythm and blues in England. The Marquee was
a jazz club right in the centre of London. People who were
heavily into jazz simply didn't dream of coming out to our
blues club way out at the end of the underground. By playing
the Marquee we had a chance to be heard by a large and
essentially different audience, and we also were working with
one of the biggest drawing bands . . . cause Chris would get
virtually a thousand people on a single night. And that kind
of set-up gave blues a really excellent exposure to the major
London music population.

Sometime before we had gotten the Ealing club going,
Mick had sent along some tapes because, y'know, there were
so few of us about that we had to get to know each other.
The first thing I knew of Mick was when he sent me this
tape of some things which he and Keith and one or two
friends had done out in Dartford. Then he came over to talk
about Bo Diddley and Chuck Berry and people like that.
He'd come over to chat all the time . . . A couple of real blues
enthusiasts, him and Keith. And, y'know, I had known Brian
Jones long before that. I met Brian in Cheltenham when I
was doing some gigging with the Chris Barber Band there.

In those days I didn't work with a regular band, y'know.
I used to go and blow with various people. Cyril and I kept
having sorta odd periods when we couldn't stand the sight of

each other. And we'd split up for six months or so, and then we'd eventually get back together again. It was during one of these periods of divorce – when I said that I couldn't stand playing at the pub on Thursday nights anymore – that I went off to blow with a jazz quartet down at the Troubadour in Old Brompton Road in Chelsea, y'know. Anyway, the drummer down there was Charlie ... Charlie Watts, y'know. And I said to him, I'm thinking about forming a band, how would you like to play drums. And he said yeah. And so he was with the very first band, the band that opened the Ealing Club. And he was also with the band that opened the Marquee. But he was replaced in the summers because he didn't want to go pro ... he had a good spot in an advertising agency and he wanted to stay put because he didn't feel that there was enough security in the music business. And so we had to let him go ... and that's how Ginger Baker came into the band.

Ginger Baker (munching on a mess of chocolate gâteau at the Cumberland Hotel at Marble Arch while Linda E. snaps away at her Nikon): 'Alexis was a cat with fantastic taste and drive ... y'know, generally you get one or the other ... somebody who can push mountains but has shit for taste or some delicate and beautiful cat with lots of taste but about the drive of a rose petal. Alexis was the exception and that's why he's the real foundation of English blues.'

Alexis: Anyway, getting back to the tapes that Mick sent along to me ... they weren't particularly good. Naturally they had no technical merits, being home-made recordings. They were very involved in the rock side of blues ... Chuck Berry and Bo Diddley. Brian was into a different kind of thing, and eventually he would influence Mick in that direction: Elmore James and Muddy Waters. Brian, in effect, brought more of the blues scene as opposed to the rock scene into what Keith and Mick were doing. Let's put it this way ... Brian brought the latter-day country thing into it. Y'know, it was a very important mixture. I recall Brian

Jones on stage at that early period . . . playing tambourine. He was by far the most evil of the lot. A very heavy scene he had going for a while.

Brian and I had known each other long before I got things together with Cyril. And Brian used to come up to Chelsea and he'd sleep on the floor. He just couldn't stand being in Cheltenham, and he'd come into London whenever he could afford it. He didn't have any money, y'know . . . like most of us. So he'd camp at my place and we'd talk about blues all the time. And I naturally had a certain interest in seeing what he eventually did on stage insofar as I had listened to his ideas for such a long time. And Brian on stage at that time was *certainly* as powerful a personality as Mick was. And in certain countries in Europe, particularly in Germany, the fans were more into a Brian Jones cult than a Mick Jagger cult . . . at that point . . . because, gradually, it shifted. It shifted partly because of Brian's pulling back . . . but the initial impact, for a lot of people, was more Brian than Mick. It's very difficult and a bit touchy to explain exactly why Brian pulled back the way he did. I think he found it very difficult to cope with the schizophrenia which is always involved when you play music professionally. He was very delicately balanced in that way, and I think he found it a bit too dangerous to deal with that kind of duality. Probably that's what eventually got to him. I saw it coming a long time ago.

Al Aronowitz: 'It was Brian who founded the Stones and discovered all those obscure black blues records by Bo Diddley and Chuck Berry and Willie Dixon that he somehow imported from America and put into the Stones' own language. "I was the undisputed leader of the group," he used to say. "The undisputed leader!" His undisputed leadership lasted only until The Stones started making enough money for it to be worthwhile for someone to dispute. Lead singer Mick Jagger and lead guitarist Keith Richard joined co-manger Andrew Loog Oldham in a coup d'état and the next thing Brian knew was the Rolling Stones were cutting two sides in L.A. without him.' [1]

[1] The *New York Post*.

Alexis: That's the nature of the music business: it's far more complex psychologically than most people realise. You have to find your balance in it rationally or it will destroy you very quickly. What I mean, of course, is that most of us have two distinct lives. I can't go into all the details, y'know, because these things are private, but the predicament is pretty obvious: you've got a life you live at home and quite another that you live on the road. The face you show the press, the fans and the face you see in the mirror . . . the one your friends see, that is, if you're lucky enough to keep any friends, isn't the same.

It would be, y'know, quite ludicrous for me to behave on the road the way I behave at home. And vice versa, of course. I keep both sides of me going . . . and I understand that it's not so much a question of a split-personality as two necessary life-styles. Obviously they are both a part of me, but I don't let them interfere with each other. It's a bit of a Jekyll and Hyde . . . for instance, I never bother much to drink at home, but on the road, if I'm really very high after playing, I'll drink a whole bottle before I go to sleep. I'm louder, more extroverted . . . I'm really very different on the road.

It's quite the same with Mick . . . a thoughtful, rather quiet bloke at home and a really outrageous personality on stage. He came from a very sedate background, Mick did . . . he's hardly a Cockney with a flair for rock 'n' roll. With a father as a college prof and his mother . . . a . . . I don't know quite what.

And he laughs . . . I remember his mother ringing me up one day: *Well, my, my . . . well, I don't know about all this singing and trying to make it in professional music for my son. Tell me, Mr Korner, do you think he has half a chance?*

And I *did* say at the time – thank god at least for that! – that I thought he was going to be an absolute smash.

And she said to me: *Well, that's very odd now isn't it. I had no idea . . . hmmmm.*

And Keith's mum too, she'd go off to look in on the boys when they eventually left home and took a flat together, and she'd be flabbergasted by the wreck and ruin of the place. Saying things like: Keith, dear, have ya brushed your teeth proper, me boy. *And Alexis laughs, enjoying the pictures which flash upon his memory.* Their parents couldn't possibly grasp the direction in which they were headed. They saw them in a completely different light. They only see one side. That just confirms my idea about pop people having dual personalities.

Mick: 'It's like when we're in Paris. It's an event, and your friends are there . . . all our parents were there. Well, it's kinda weird doin' that bump and grind to me mum, y'know. I just feel pretty weird.'

Alexis: Brian, for instance, existed in a life entirely different from the one which his parents might expect of him. He had lots of hangups. One of the most recurrent – and probably a basis for his withdrawing from the leadership of the Stones – was this notion of his that he was making it on his looks and not his music. It was very strange . . . and it was impossible to get it through to him that making it on any basis in a field as insane as the music business was just as justifiable as making it any other way. But that's just another aspect of the old schizophrenia – one side of you doubts your abilities, motives, talents . . . everything . . . one side doubts everything about the other side of you.

David Dalton: '*Thursday night at the Marquee was blues night, and Alexis' group, with Mick as vocalist, was the house band. At that time there was a weekly TV programme of jazz on the BBC, and Alexis' Blues Incorporated was to be the featured group. However, the BBC did not consider Mick a jazz vocalist, and insisted that John Baldry take his place for the programme.*'

Alexis: Now the audience is not terribly unlike the performer insofar as these people are one thing in the hall while the music's going on, and they're quite another thing when they go off quietly home. They allow themselves this dual personality, but they absolutely will not tolerate the notion that Mick Jagger doesn't eat dinner at home the same way that he sings 'Bitch' on stage. It's a very peculiar situation when you finally arrive at the situation where you can dictate the nature of everything surrounding your public image. Mick's a very clever boy – apart from being a very talented one – and much of what has come of his career was carefully planned and thought out by him. It's no accident. Not in the least. And I can recall him before all the publicity as being a ... how should I put it? ... *fairly outrageous one*. And I was more than a bit amazed that he was hanging on at the London School of Economics. Even at that time Mick had already made a sorta fetish out of hair. For instance, first time I saw him work, he'd swing his head around and make his hair fly. It was really very early for that particular kind of showmanship, at least in London it was. Remarks were made, naturally. Because you have to understand that a man with hair long enough to be tossed and tussled was very very *strange* in those days. This was the first time for any of us in England to be working with someone who was deliberately theatrical ... but don't misunderstand. Other singers had been showy and all. In fact, John Baldry, well now, John used to be theatrical, but theatrical in the way that the old vaudevillian stars were theatrical. Sort of corny and homely, if y'know what I mean.

Mick: '*There are two important things about* Performance – *there's the sexual thing, not only physically sexual, but the inter-relating of the sexes and the interchange of roles. And the role of violence and the role of women, vis-à-vis the role of violence of a man. How the two things can balance each other out ... the whole thing of films is a cheat. It's all illusion and an illusion on top of other illusions. There's so many illusions that I've forgotten after a while.*'

Alexis: Mick had a very different kind of showmanship, and he was different from the very beginning. One of the most interesting things about Mick as a personality, and it's a very delicate subject, is the enormous impact he has made on the world when it comes to male identification. He's

basically helped to alter the whole idea of what it is to be male. He personally may not have done it, but his example has been a very, very strong one. I think you can imagine just how shocking Mick was in the early days when you consider that the kind of theatricality which Mick uses is not really the kind of mannerism which you easily identify with the male role in the theatre. It's more of a kinda Marilyn Monroe thing. And, frankly, it was wildly embarrassing first time 'round with it. I'll tell you frankly that there were definitely schisms between Mick and Cyril on occasions, and they weren't really musical ones although Cyril would have insisted they were. They were based on behaviour really – not music. Over behaviour patterns ... on stage. Cyril, y'know, was very old school. Very straight and heavy. I mean, a typical Cyril Davies announcement would run something like this: This - is - a - blues - by - John - Lee - Hooker - and - if - you - don't - think - he - was - the - best - blues - picker - ever - you - need - your fucking - head - examined. . . . Without smile, without theatre ... so that it becomes heavy theatre. Mick, of course, was totally something else. And the odd spats they had – and there weren't very many – I'm convinced were over behaviour and not music.

You see, Cyril and I never could agree about where rock and roll started and blues finished. Because I didn't feel that there could be any specific termination points for things like that, whereas Cyril did. And he felt that we were doing too much rock and roll and not enough blues. He connected Mick's stage mannerisms with what he didn't like about rock and roll. He was one of the blues purists who is inclined in the direction of jazz and a small appreciative audience rather than towards pop and a large audience. He *definitely* understood what Mick was attempting, but it was a matter of the old school not approving of the new school. With Mick and Cyril it was very friendly – but the purists in great numbers who eventually disapproved of Mick were not very nice about it and consequently were largely responsible for holding up the Stones' success for such a long time. But don't misunderstand what I mean. At no time, from those earliest days till now, have I ever heard anybody indulge in cruel jokes about Mick's behaviour. The band never got into that and nobody else that I ever worked with ever indulged in that sort of thing. I don't believe that any of us ever thought of it in that way. For us Mick had something in common with Bill Haley. What I mean is that the thing which made Bill Haley memorable for British audiences was the way newspapers handled stories about the ripping up of theatre seats during his performances. That sort of publicity gets through to the public. In Mick's unconventional behaviour there was a presumption by the audience of anarchy and therefore of inherent violence.

That image has persisted throughout his career. There's another kind of thing which Mick does which isn't at all like anything connected with Bill Haley. That's a kind of outrage which is very similar to somebody like Little Richard. I don't know why Mick can do it so much better than Richard. But he can. ... After all, I don't know how many really good spade drag acts I've seen in my life. That's where the problem is now, isn't it. Anyway, it's a bit strange that Mick picked Bo and Chuck Berry as his idols rather than Little Richard. But I can understand when I think back on Mick in those days. He picked Chuck cause of the lyrics – which were pure, absolutely pure Americanisms. And Bo Diddley for that very, very heavy country rhythm. Little Richard, y'see, was already a whole thing. Excess was his thing, y'know, so where could you go from there? One of my favourite albums is 'Rill thing' ... but what do you do for an encore? It's rather like Django Reinhart in jazz.

Mick was very, very involved in what he was doing. But he realised that one of the very few ways of retaining your sanity when you're that committed is with the ability to laugh at yourself. It's an English tradition to be disrespectful ... we rather enjoy poking fun at things. And Mick simply took this a bit farther ... finding the absurdity not only in the world but in his own life as well. He always had a rather nasty laugh, so he's carried it farther.

In those days it really didn't occur to anyone that we were involved in what was essentially an imitative kind of music. Now, of course, you can go back and realise how awful some of the imitation was. We all were derivative to the extent that we had taken the music from a country we didn't know ... we deliberately focused on Afro-American music which was racially removed from us ... what we learned was from hearsay and there was a lot of the intimate detail of the inner-soul of this music which we didn't get via phonograph records ... which were our principal source of getting to know American blues. Because, after all, we didn't know what it was really like to be American. Mick and Keith had these fantasies which became very real after a while, but they were just fantasies ... *real* fantasies, but fantasies all the same. We could only get into this kind of music by way of such fantasies and imitation. But it was a real thing – something which got home even here in England. And so it was true – it was a true music in the long run, if you see what I mean.

One of the big criticisms of Joplin was the accusation that she tried to sound like a spade when she wasn't one. But that's such an unimportant point except insofar as it showed up the irony of black performers who couldn't make it with their own music just because they were black, y'know. But the important thing about Janis wasn't whether she was black, green or lavender ... what was important was the fact that she moved people.

Alexis: Yes, quite.

But, I must admit, that one also thinks about the fact that she came from Fort Arthur, Texas ... did grow up with this music all around her ... but I've also thought: like, y'know, what's the difference really between being a white chick living in Fort Arthur and living in West London and having this same music on your phonograph day and night? You're still growing up in a blues environment whether you've prefabbed it or whether it's natural.

67

Alexis: Yes, it's perfectly true. It's the same argument that we always presented to our half-million critics who always carped on that native roots point-of-view. Quite a bore, really, and very much beside the point. We kept getting it thrown at us: me, Mick, Brian, everybody . . . y'know, they'd say . . . you're not black, you're not American, you can't possibly understand this music, so why don't you leave it alone. But an environment is a purely emotional thing, having little to do with facts. It's something which is created in your own head. But, I'll admit, we personally had to learn to believe that . . . rationally and not just emotionally . . . before we could understand our purpose and also argue our way with the purists who were everywhere. It's a shame that artists have to spend so much of their time justifying what they are doing and what they have accomplished rather than simply accomplishing more of it. It can also increase your duality to get into justifications all the time. Soon you become a part-time parlour-room intellectual . . . telling the ladies what it's all about, and the rest of the time you're a dance-hall exhibitionist. That could get to be kinda displacing after a while.

Mick and I tend to agree on several points, I think. One of them, obviously, is the fact that we don't feel the least need to justify ourselves to absolutely anybody. And though that may seem rather ordinary in the world of pop, actually it was a breakthrough for Mick and the boys. If you see what I mean . . . for instance, if you consider the way that Brian Epstein handled the Beatles: the constant apology, the constant inference that despite everything 'they're really nice, clean polite kids'. The Stones are quite in contrast to that attitude. What the Stones really have done from the beginning . . . and it's unbelievably honest for a field like the music business . . . what Mick and the others have done is insist that one's personal attitude, mannerisms, sex life and everything else are nobody's business. Without making announcements, declarations, confessions or justifications, the Stones have always gone about the business of being the Stones. Denying nothing, admitting nothing. Adding immeasurably to the Stones' myth and reality, both at the same time. And through all of this, Mick has amazingly kept his sanity. He's willing to be more than he is, willing to get credit for more than he's done, willing to be held responsible for worse and better than he's intentionally achieved. That's a kind of sanity, really. And as such I think Mick has socially emancipated a business, by *really* and *truly* depreciating the value of sentimentality as opposed to sentiment. Everything about Mick testifies to this very, very important achievement. He has successfully turned a new eye towards the world: looking upon it in his lyrics, in his mannerisms, poses, attitudes, in all ways he looks upon it with disrespect but with love. It's a delicate combination – one which many people misinterpret. It's the prime virtue of a film like *Performance* because it captures, fictionally but realistically, this quality of disrespect and love which motivates Mick.

Coda: Go back to letter A for the processional music and go out in 4/4 time on the high hat; slow fade.

Exiles On Main Street

In the middle of the intersection, framed by three gas stations and a TacO StanD, Dominique rolled his red bandana and tied it around his head. When the light changed he took off down Sports Arena Boulevard, San Diego, on top of his funky old motorcycle, which farted out its uneven exhaust underneath him. It was a bitchen day – his tyres hissing along, sunny-side-up on the griddle-hot asphalt. A really bitchen day! Burning a halo around his massive, curly locks. Sending lazy rivers down his neck and chest, and burnishing him into a fine umber finish.

Ramada Inn, the Yucca Hotel, Holiday Inn and the Seven Seas Hyatt Lodge – all in a row – saluting Dominique and the horde of military foundlings who plunge along Hotel Circle in borrowed *woodies* – those immaculate 1954 jobs by Ford: sturdy station wagons, armoured in wood. Debris from those preposterous years when men were men and wagons didn't have prefabricated-real-imitation-fine-grain-embossed-panels. This is the real thing. Cigarette lighter, heater, defrost, shortwave radio and a rear, left-hand door that hasn't opened from the inside ever since the day that Alan Rupert got wiped out by a lot of heavy water at Windansea Beach.

Of course that was a bummer. For Dominique it was really terrible because he and Alan had been virtually inseparable. Everywhere you went you'd see the two of them hanging out together, staring at surfboards in shop windows, staring at a chick in the White Whale or just plain staring off into space when they flew along in their woodie. Getting their kicks on Interstate 5. Ocean Beach, Pacific Beach, Mission Beach, then La Jolla. Or if they got really horny and wanted to fuckhelloutta some chick, you'd see 'm in Tijuana or maybe Baja. In a little room with terrifyingly large roses all over the walls, in an old bed that yowledand-groaned with lumpy bruises every time they lunged at the chubby Senorita. Two Dollar. Making so fuckin' much noise that he could hardly keep his hard-on and she just sat back and wiped her mouth.

'Why you neber like do it in me?' she mexicated flatly, while the guys haunched in front of her, staring at her enormous tits and insistently jerking off in the silence. 'You never want it in me . . .!' she complains as she waddles across the little room and squats on the pot. 'Sumthun not good yous two. *Hoy! Me siento deprimida . . . pesadillas . . . estoy mala . . . adios . . .*'

But Alan's gone now, under tons of white water.

His board was quietly slipped back up on the strand by the gentle cascade, but his body was forever retained by the monstrous surf. . . . And so, of course, Alan Rupert wasn't on line to catch the Stone's concert. He wasn't around when *Exiles on Main Street* was released, so Dominique had to try to turn on to it all by himself, sitting with his cassette in the Tourmaline Canyon storm drain or in Balboa Park, and trying to work up Alan's madness for the Stones. Trying to imagine what Alan would say, what Alan would feel. How Alan would laugh that marvellous laugh. How Alan would get very serious and bite the nail of his thumb and listened for the spaces between the words which Dominique could never hear. 'What we're gonna do as soon as we get it together, man,' Alan would always say, 'what we're gonna do is, see we're gonna get in a VW or even the woodie if that's the best we can do, and Dom, you and me, like man, we're gonna just set out and follow their whole fuckin' tour and, y'know, sit there clean across the United States of America just fucking groovin' on all that good shit and see if, y'know, Mick can *really* keep it up, I mean *really* keep everybody's head flying like that, man, what a fuckin' blast. . . .'

But Alan was gone. And it was rough on Dominique. He had gotten a lot more sullen and he didn't go to Tijuana anymore. Without Alan it wasn't fun anymore . . . even if he got stoned out of his mind he still couldn't get into it without Alan.

He moved out of the garage where Cathy and three guys from Santa Barbara had set up housekeeping and where they threw really crazy parties. All the sudden they just seemed like kids to Dominique, and he hated the way they did this game about lowering their voices when they talked about Alan. *Getting points for his death, y'know; like it means shit to them, man. Like they fuckin' cared shit about anything but their fucking rock'n' roll!*

Tu apetencia de muerte y el gusto de su boca. . . . The Senorita Two Dollar she sings in his surfing nightmares. Her tits afloat. A trillion bubbles flowing steadily from her nostrils as a constant creamy white exhaust overflows from between her legs, like ink from an octopus. And now . . . she floats slowly away, towed on pink nylon cords by a fleet of cock-shaped flying fish. *Adios, la Senorita Dos Pesos, adios.*

It's a bitchen day. Sex-California-hot, everything heating up. Beer and wine, reds and acid, swimmingpoolmadness. It's a bitchen day. The plastic seat burning up under his glorious God-given ass – as he zips past 'That Place', where the San Diego State playmates devour beer and peanuts and occasionally stagger next door to the Go-Kart joint for a crashing bore. Then over to Boll-Weevil where Dominique rolls up briefly for a cheeseburger *with everything, please, and don't grill the onions, y'hear?* The waitress is one of those neon-light-ladies who doesn't register recognition and limits her essays to 'What'll-ya-have' while she stares relentlessly beyond your left ear and screws up her mouth and adjusts the big handkerchief in her breastpocket.

Next a raunchy phalanx of bikers rally around the parking lot. A hungry horde of metallic flies, buzzing the curb and collecting noisily around this Baby Doll chick from Fresno with white hair and big calves in white majorette boots. The bikers boil slowly. From within their quilted leather jackets comes a beasty fume into the 105-Dago-air. They celebrate every touchdown in their California highway scrimmage. Laying on of hands to heal the teenie-chicklets of suburbia. Raggy rhinoes ... cumbrous, explosive, unpredictable. Yet ever so delicate ... an ego floating like a yoke on a slightly fried egg. Very easily broken.

'They're strictly servant-claass,' Dominique tells the waitress, 'but, why not, they're very heavy cats.' In the abstract they're the Brechtian proletarians, the natural heirs of Brando, Dean and General George S. Patton. 'So they're okay, y'see, if they're sitting six rows back.' Dominique laughs and then smiles to himself: that's the kind of thing Alan would have said. R. D. Laing would say: '*If our experience is destroyed, our behaviour will be destructive.*'

United Press International said: *Thousands of persons tried to crash the gates of a performance last night by the Rolling Stones rock group.*

Actually there were maybe five hundred kids with Molotovs and Coke bottles. The Tactical Squad – looking amazingly like dry-cleaned bikers – moved out and cleared up the rioters like a new Hoover Vacuum. They even brought in the sanitation department to hose off the debris. And now nothing's left but the big CHEVY sign rotating slowly over 696,769 San Diegans who sleep under the watchful eye of 902 policemen in their home of the brave and their land of the free.

CRIMINAL INTELLIGENCE
INFORMATION REPORT

Classification: General   *File:* Miscellaneous
Reference: Rolling Stones Concert

Informant advised writer that University of New Mexico students were afraid to go to the concert. Informant stated that everyone who was *straight* was afraid because the concert was supposed to be the start

73

of a riot in this city. Informant reported he was told, 'We didn't get our riot in May so we'll get it in June.'

The American Southwest is rapidly becoming the burial ground of the proud indigenous inhabitants of the western hemisphere. It is also becoming the multimillion-dollar sepulcher of a vast geriatric tribe. Cliff-dwellers of the multitiered concrete pueblos which annually rise out of the pathetic bit of reclaimed earth in this otherwise cruel landscape. Not all the elephants have come to die. Some have come simply to visit the hysterically homey string of dude ranches which dig their nails into the soft white underbelly of Indian turf. The dignified natives – Papago, Navajo, Pima, Hopi, Zuni – watch with mixed emotions as the tides of retired shopkeepers descend upon them. Retired mothers from the generation of TV-Dinner-Housewives who learned how to use electric can openers in home economics at P.S. 21, in 1946. In sensible black shoes out of which grow forty-four-year-old legs. Complete with vein-charted sub-white ankles. Flaccid flesh squeezing like sour cream in plastic sacks out of Macy's $3.99 sunsuits. Thighs tie-dyed with faded yellow bruises, tinged with tiny purple veins. Los Angeles goggle-sunglasses. A simulated human hair blonde wighat topped preposterously by a Katharine Hepburn floppy sunhat. And on the faces that creamy, thick, beige death mask which they methodically putty into the cracks and which they smear hopefully over their throats which are in the terrifying process of becoming flesh draperies. Faces that look like unmade beds.

The shopkeeper has crucified and carried this little lady through thirty years of holy mattress-moany. They have skillfully reduced each other to very agreeable vegetables in that little cottage in suburban New Jersey which they recently sold to newlyweds for four times what they paid for it. Hubby wears a brown hat in the midday sun and sandals with semitransparent, black anklet socks. And he's got his Instamatic and AAA tripticks and thermos. And the big

Dodge with the American flag decal on the windshield, and Venetian blinds on the back window.

'My kids is grown and in college and I figure that they better live their own lives no matter what I think about it,' daddy says. 'What the hell, I can't figure out all this nonsense with long hair and loud music and whathaveyou, but I figure they'll outgrow it!'

Saying his piece and then heartily listening with his whole face. Laughing when there's no reason to laugh and repeating everything you say with that very serious tone which is usually reserved for Thanksgiving and the Fourth of July. He's learned not to talk about niggers, commies or kikes. He loves to give you the elbow in the ribs and fill you in on a joke. And he likes getting that righteous look on his face when there's mixed company and when it becomes vulgar to tell the same joke. *Take care! Here comes the little lady. Don't want to shock mama, y'know.* Or he likes to push back in his red naugahide-reclining TV-chair with a cigarette:

Warning: The Surgeon General Has Determined
That Cigarette Smoking Is Dangerous to Your Health

and speculate with the other ex-shopkeepers about the country's future. Shocked profoundly by gossip concerning young Kennedy *and that poor girl who got mysteriously drowned in that damn river. Or that there funny fella-ah-Jenkins.* But apparently unshocked by the Watergate Affair.

'Now I tell you that if kids are going to be violent they've got to be taught a lesson or there just won't be any stopping them. That's the trouble with us – we just spoil the heck out of our kids in America. Now my father. . . .'

Mick Jagger saw none of this. By the time he was airborne, they were conducting an investigation to discover who was responsible for the *preplanned disobedience* in San Diego, and the forces of Tucson were dumping tear gas and Mace into the crowd of two hundred fifty rowdy Arizonians outside

75

the hall where the Stones gave one quick ride around the course and took off for Albuquerque.

The Criminal Intelligence Information Report issued in New Mexico suggested that the enormous Spanish population of Albuquerque was going to show up in force without tickets and would cause trouble if they were turned away at the concert.

Tour manager Peter Rudge spun off into hysteria and leaped to local promoter Barry Fey's aid, organising a mammoth defence programme. They co-ordinated *three* police forces – city, state and campus – and marched out into the streets of beautiful downtown Albuquerque prepared for a civil war. What they found was an orderly crowd which shuffled off to the Stones' Barmitzvah without a single incident. Immediately thereafter, the Stones and Company packed it up and, dashing through the dust, took one long glance backward and said: 'So that's Albuquerque . . . very interesting.'

'Brian . . . y'know, he was the one who kept us all together in the early days. 'Cause Mick, y'see, he was still going to school,' Keith Richard said.

It's 1962 and the shiny-faced Beach Boys are working out the changes for a new tune called *Surfin' U.S.A.* Patty Duke's a child in a spectacularly dramatic flick called *The Miracle Worker*. Tom Hayden's SDS Manifesto is mimeographed and passed quietly around the colleges. Marilyn slips away, and Dean Rusk reports on the horrifying Cuban Missile Crisis: 'We're eyeball to eyeball, and I think the other fellow just blinked.'

The good folks are fox-trotting to 'Moon River'. The people who think they're hep are pantomiming David Rose's 'The Stripper'. Meanwhile lots of kids and black folks are pushing along to Ray Charles' 'I Can't Stop Loving You' and to Joey Dee and the Starlighters' 'Peppermint Twist'.

Ralph Ginzburg gets busted for *Eros* magazine. James

76

Meredith becomes the first spade at U of Mississippi. Vassar President Sarah Gibson Blanding called a compulsory assembly where she told her 1,450 girl-students to stay chaste or leave the campus. On Broadway, Edward Albees' *Who's Afraid of Virginia Woolf?* is assassinating the American marital institution. And Brian, Keith and Mick Jagger have left home and found a flat in London. 'We decided to live in London to get it together. Time to break loose. So everybody left home, upped and got this tragic pad in London. In Chelsea. Just Mick, myself and Brian,'[1] Keith explains.

Chelsea – the orderly British version of the Sunset Strip – was already becoming the dry-dock of London's professional fanatics and persistent dingos. It's in the West – a district of old areas with drastic separation between ghettos and garden squares. Notting Hill to the north is the nearest London comes to a Greenwich Village with its heavy concentration of beatniks and West Indians. But in 1962, the squalor began to outweigh the funkiness.

'We had the middle floor,' Keith remembers.

One night, after doing a fantastic beggars' banquet of fish and chips, which was bought from the proceeds of selling beer bottles, Mick, Brian and Keith were playing a Muddy Waters' album. One of the treasures brought by the post from Chicago, Illinois, U.S.A. 'What's that?' Mick yelled during the 'Rolling Stones' track. 'Man, wouldn't that make a fuckin' farout name!' Enlarging upon Muddy, the three musicians decided to call themselves the Silver Rolling Stones. *Late fantasy tripping*.

Now they have fallen out in corners of their semifurnished flat. A truck rattles by . . . a singing drunk . . . as they sleep. Then it's silent. The sun starts to pry at the draped windows. But there's no movement. Until all the sudden Mick comes flying out of bed, muttering and shuffling as he tries to get himself dressed and out of the apartment in time for his first class at the London School of Economics.

'Jesus, what's the panic!' Keith mutters without coming out from under his pillow.

[1] Rolling Stones.

Jagger ignores him and checks his downy beard. He figures he can wait another few days before shaving. He quickly pampers the locks which are descending over his ears and collar and then rattles down the stairs. His roommates open an eye and scrutinise the kettle which still has a bit of steam left in it after Mick's hurried morning tea. As they creep from their bed there's the steady silence of slumber from the floor below.

'Downstairs,' Keith recalls, 'downstairs was livin' four old whores from Liverpool. Isn't that a coincidence. . . .'

' 'allo dahlin', 'ow are ya? Awright?' she says as she putters around the hallway, searching for her key. 'Luve-ly weeeatha we'ire 'avin', now ain't-tit!'

Jagger's scholarship funds were the only regular source of money. 'Sometimes we'd get invited to a party,' Keith says, 'and that was a high spot because it meant that we could get a drink or two, or at least a snack. Like, I reckon that a lot of musicians have to starve for their art, but honest! . . . I mean, our situation was ridiculous.' And he laughs. 'We'd go round these parties, y'know, and wait for an opportunity to examine the inside of the fridge. If no one was looking, we'd try to lift a couple of eggs or something . . . then hide them away so we could get them away without them breaking. We had to become petty pilferers. I mean, now that's pretty deplorable!'

'Deplorable, indeed,' Mrs Humber says emphatically, shaking her dust mop into the hallway and frowning. 'I remember them fellas very well indeed, always havin' that music so bleedin' loud, they did. Night and day and in between times too, they just went at it full time.' And she smiles confidently: 'But they was nice lads actually. I remember thinkin' how homeless and wretched they were, poor little things. Skinny and shaggy like old dogs. And they obviously weren't accustomed to the hard life, y'know; I mean they was obvious from good families and the like, and it wasn't fittin' for them to be livin' in such a place as this neighbourhood in *those* days. Now, me, I've been livin' in this very flat here my whole life. I was born right here and my old mother, God bless her, died right here in these rooms. We put her to rest five years ago this July, poor love. She was a strong woman, y'know, without a fearful bone in 'er body. "That Mick fella," she'd tell me, "now that's a nice boy and a talented one too." But poor darlin' never lived to see them become stars. Died in the summer of 1962, she did. . . .'

While Mrs Humber was burying her mother, the Stones were playing their first gig at Ealing, without Charlie Watts. 'Our first breakthrough,' says Keith, 'was when we got the job of deputising for Alexis Korner.'

'They were very rough at that point,' Alexis recalls. 'But audiences clearly liked them. It's difficult to explain what it was all about . . . but these boys were different, and people were tired of the trad bands and welcomed something new. Besides there was the fantastic magic of Brian's stage presence and that amazing frenetic theatricality of Jagger, driving lyrics into a cheap microphone and shaking his hair and prancing like nothing we'd ever seen before.'

Their minimal success was greeted with the scorn of the people who formed a tiny jazz élite in London. They were outraged by the intrusion of performers whom they considered primitive, imitative and personally repulsive. Jagger was agonised by the cool-rage of these dilettantes who conspicuously ignored the Stones.

'They made up a small élite of writers, musicians, club owners and old-timers,' Jagger recalls. The world of jazz was their social scene and their special ego-trip. For years this musical expression of the American black had provided them with a basis for musical superiority. Out of every dozen English jazz fans there were perhaps two or three who really liked the music. The rest found in the identification with jazz a bohemianism not unlike that of the art collectors of Paris. They liked the cloistered separatism of their tiny world of music and they didn't want it intruded upon by the likes of the Rolling Stones or fancypants Jagger.

Jagger was continually attacked. 'I don't want to go into detail because it's not fashionable at the moment to spell it

79

out, but Jagger was absolutely intolerable. His mannerisms and his attitude were repulsive in the truest sense of that word. I know people who were simply too *embarrassed* to watch his exhibitionism. And the music which he was trying to pass off as authentic blues was a mixture of the worst of American urban popular songs and English Teddy Boyism,' a Marquee regular remembers. 'I think everybody also felt that it was a clear disgrace that a group looking like *that* – I mean, so ungroomed and totally unacceptable – should make money out of the jazz world. It was a disgrace!'

These attitudes were a subtle but overwhelming obstacle in the path of Mick Jagger and his friends. The people who owned the clubs were always being told that they should steer clear of these blues-fakes. These owners were not inclined to offend the taste of their regular clients despite the fact that they noticed that the Stones had a growing group of young fans. Meanwhile the journals and musical tabloids which are essential to the success of a musical group were dominated by strict traditionalists who felt that white Europeans had a right to jazz (inasmuch as it was a marriage of Afro-American folk music and European symphonic music), but the blues, they insisted, was a native folk form, and it was as ridiculous for a white English kid to sing the blues as it was for him to do the hula. They failed to mention that this theory would also prove that it was ridiculous for an American born Greek soprano named Callas to sing Italian and French opera; for an Osage Indian named Tallchief to dance in Russian ballets, or for a Portuguese kid named John Dos Passos to write a great American novel.

'To hell with the lot of them,' Mick yelled. 'We'll just keep hammering away. We'll make it in spite of that lot. From now on, we'll work harder than ever. Anyone who doesn't like us can do the other thing. . . .'[1]

But Mick's war-cry didn't change the situation. The Stones were getting nowhere. They had a monthly gig at Ealing and an occasional spot at the Marquee where they were eagerly ignored. People would intentionally move back

[1] Rolling Stones.

and forth in front of the platform and collect in groups and laugh and talk loudly.

When Mick wasn't braving the bold indifference of the London snobs he and his friends were batting out tunes at a little club near Watford where a handful of people showed up and sat placidly while Jagger churned up the atmosphere.

On Boxing Day, 1962 – that peculiar English holiday immediately following Christmas – the boys were booked at the Piccadilly Club in London. It turned out to be the perfect disaster with which to end an already horrendous year.

Nobody moved. Nobody clapped. The audience sat stoically, staring blankly at the Stones and trying to figure out what the hell Jagger was doing and what kind of song he was singing. His wild, uninhibited blues style and his mumbled phrases and bodily gyrations left them on the verge of hilarity. But something about Mick's intensity prevented them from laughing. The audience was half humiliated and half horrified. Glancing at each other they got more and more uncomfortable, more and more silent.

After the set, the audience filed out mumbling. The promoter shut out the lights and pushed the door closed, only glancing at Jagger with a sullen 'Goodnight. . . .'

'It was about that time,' Charlie Watts recalls, 'that they asked me to kick in with them. Honestly, I thought they were mad. I mean, they were working a lot of dates without even getting paid or even worrying about it. And there was me, earning a pretty comfortable living with the Korner band, which obviously was going to nose dive if I got involved with these crazy Stones. It made me laugh to think of them, even trying to get me in with them. But, y'know, I got to thinking about it. My biggest mistake! And, well, I liked their spirit and I was getting very involved in rhythm 'n' blues. I figured it would be a bit of an experiment for me and a bit of a challenge, too. So I said OK, yes, I'd join. Lots of my friends, y'know, thought I'd gone stark raving . . . see, the thing with me is that I'm not really much of a worrier. Only thing that had me wondering, once I'd made up my mind, was the fact that the Stones were so disliked inside the jazz world. I mean, people just never stopped putting them down. It was like some sort of snobbish game they played. And half of them that did all the bitching had never even heard the band. But it was one of those things – the Stones were just a set-up. I'd heard people talking about them constantly – and it's true to say nobody had a good word for them. They were complete outsiders. Nobody wanted to know about their music because everybody was too busy looking on them as just a gang of long-haired freaks.'[1]

The year 1963 opens with Alabama Governor George C. Wallace: 'I draw the line in the dust and toss the gauntlet before the feet of tyranny and I say segregation now, segregation tomorrow, segregation forever!' James Baldwin counters with a constant shower of literary triumphs while Betty Friedan publishes *The Feminine Mystique*, which gives birth to the New Woman. The four-cent Lincoln postage stamp disappears and the five-cent George Washington variety becomes standard equipment on all first-class letters.

Quang Duc, a seventy-three-year-old Buddhist monk, transforms his body into a torch to protest the régime of Ngo Dinh Diem, and Maxwell Taylor and Robert McNamara declare that 'the major part of the United States military task can be completed by the end of 1965'. Mayor Richard Daley announces that 'there are no ghettos in Chicago!' and 'Limbo Rock' by Chubby Checker is the number one tune of the year while Tony Bennett persists with 'I Left My Heart in San Francisco'. In rapid succession John F. Kennedy is assassinated, Lee Harvey Oswald is executed, and Lyndon B. Johnson becomes president of the United States of America.

'I had been moving through this scene at Richmond ... y'know, at Surrey,' Brian said. 'I had gone out there to hear this Dave Wood Rhythm and Blues Band which worked at this little club called Crawdaddy, just over the road from the railway station at Richmond. Well, they weren't much, but the club owner was sorta a gas.' He was

[1] Rolling Stones.

bearded Giorgio Gomelsky, an old-school bohemian eccentric with the accent of a White Russian and the flamboyant nomenclature of a film documentary producer/promoter. His manner was over-rich . . . echoing a Hollywood mogul down to the trim of his jacket and the glint in his eyes. But he had successfully promoted the National Blues Festival that was the first event to introduce Chicago blues performers to England and he had done a good job of keeping the atmosphere at the Crawdaddy authentic and cool.

'Dave Wood's group,' Brian recalled, 'was going to leave for one reason or another and I heard that this Gomelsky was looking for a replacement. Now it had always seemed to me that what we needed was a place of our own, y'know. I mean, we needed somewhere to settle in and get it on . . . instead of rushing around all the time and hustling gigs, fighting off the jazz fans who were always at our throats. Grubbing for food like stray dogs day and night . . . lord, sometimes it was so rotten. . . . Well, anyway, I said to Mick, *you ought to get on the telephone, matie, and talk to this Gomelsky fella. You're the one who can tell 'em how good we are . . . y'know, lay it on him!*'

Jagger's vision of the triumph of the Stones was so intense that he readily took up the challenge and called Giorgio at the Station Hotel. 'Hello, is that Mr Gomelsky speaking?'

'Yesss, yesss,' came the heavily accented voice.

'Well, sir, this is Mick Jagger of the Rolling Stones, sir. . . .'

'Zhis must be telepathy,' Gomelsky shouted. 'Mick, I was going to call you! Yez, I was, zhis very day I was goin' to calling you to see if maybe you would care to coming here to Richmond and taking over zah sessions. . . .'

The fee started at one pound per man per night . . . or about two dollars. That was increased shortly thereafter to fifty percent of the take or one pound per man – whichever was higher. For Mick it was a perfect set-up because he had such firm belief that given half a chance to grow as performers and to gather an audience, the Stones would be a hit. It's a conviction shared by every half-ass band in the world. 'But these boys were really good,' Giorgio recalls. And sure enough, the crowd grew from a handful to a small group and the boys were taking in a bit above their one-pound minimum. Soon a line started forming at the Crawdaddy long before the doors opened. By Easter it looked like the Stones had an audience!

Each Sunday afternoon the Stones would show up at this Thames River resort area, utter monsters roaming this quaint weekend playground. The old gentlemen with fishing rods and the ladies with calf-bound volumes of Lord Tennyson would shrink from them as they strolled past, en route to the little club where they were anxiously awaited. Mick didn't mind the stares anymore, in fact they rather pleased him. And he would press his hand to his hip and lean a bit forward as he whistled and trucked on by the geriatric renegades.

Inside the club the atmosphere had become something unique to the music world. Giorgio had never seen anything quite like it. The ragged, undisciplined temperament of Jagger infused the audience with a profound freedom. The kids assembled in front of Mick and watched him the way they would intently stare at a magician, waiting for his sleight-of-hand if they were disbelievers or, if they were already converts, waiting like disciples before an evangelist to be exorcised to the skies. As Mick built the trance, combining motion and music like a dervish dancer, the audience was carried into itself: to the very threshold of abandon. For some, it was the ultimate sexual trip. For others it was nirvana . . . an ecstasy beyond physicality. For some it was the marginal world of uninhibited sadism, and their horror-show would bloom like some forbidden passion play. Mick led them into this fecund level of themselves. What emerged was simply whatever they were. Some of it was uproariously joyous – giving birth to crazy fandangos and endless boogies. Some of it was dank and distressing, ferocious and cruel, giving birth to recrimination and self-contempt.

Gomelsky's sensibility is essentially that of a documentary film-maker, and so this exhibition at the Crawdaddy was a natural for his camera. He couldn't think of when he had seen such an obvious subject for a film sequence. So he started filming the sessions, putting together a twenty-minute film which eventually got wide distribution and helped the Stones immeasurably in communicating their strange frenetic powers to a wide audience.

Mick has always emphasised that he gets totally engrossed in his performance but also comes out of it very quickly. He is the triumphant Caruso, slouching off the stage with great tears still pouring from his Pagliacci-eyes as he curses the audience for holding back. Instantly reborn out of the illusion of performance into the business of reality. 'I think it's fine and well for us to be out here in Richmond, but we can't just wait for the world to discover us! We've got to do something about it!' Giorgio did it. He contacted a musical journalist named Peter Jones who came out to see the boys one Sunday and was sufficiently impressed to go back to London and convince Norman Jopling of the *Record Mirror* to review the group.

The Jopling article was the first Rolling Stones review.

THE ROLLING STONES – GENUINE R AND B

As the trad scene gradually subsides, promoters of all kinds of teen-beat entertainments heave a long sigh of relief that they have found something to take its place. It's rhythm 'n' blues, of course – the number of R and B clubs that have suddenly sprung up is nothing short of fantastic.

At the Station Hotel, Kew Road, the hip kids throw themselves about to the new 'jungle music' like they never did in the more restrained days of trad.

And the combo they writhe and twist to is called the Rolling Stones. Maybe you've never heard of them – if you live far from London, the odds are you haven't.

But by gad you will! The Stones are destined to be the biggest group in the R and B scene – if that scene continues to flourish. Three months ago only fifty people turned up to see the group. Now promoter Gomelsky has to close the doors at an early hour – with over four hundred fans crowding the hall.

Those fans quickly lose their inhibitions and contort themselves to truly exciting music. Fact is that, unlike all the other R and B groups worthy of the name, the Rolling Stones have a definite visual appeal. They aren't like the jazzmen who were doing trad a few months ago and who had converted their act to keep up with the times. They are genuine R and B fanatics themselves and they sing and play in a way that one would have expected more from a colour U.S. group than a bunch of wild, exciting white boys who have the fans screaming and listening to them.

Andrew Loog Oldham is a professional delinquent . . . madcap-maverick-malchick. Modishly dead-serious and hopelessly hip, irreverent and brittle and brilliant. With a fantastic hunger for perversity and notoriety. Big-game hunter in the jungle music world of London. Part-time publicist and full-time Malenky Raskazz!

The Jopling review of the Stones plus a bit of prodding from Peter Jones led nineteen-year-old Oldham to the office of his boss, Eric Easton, an elder show-biz agent with offices in Regent Street. 'I've heard about a group down at Richmond,' Andy said calculatedly, 'who might make it big. George Harrison of the Beatles has been down with a couple of the others and actually seen them. He's doing a quiet rave about the music they play and it seems they stand a big chance of becoming a big-hit outfit. . . .'

Oldham and Easton took in the Stones in Richmond and the following day they signed them to a management contract.

'Andrew didn't know anything about blues,' Mick says flatly. 'The cat who really got the production together was Ron Marlow, the engineer for Chess. He had been on all the original sessions.'

But Oldham was a media-manipulator. He liked music but he knew very little about how it was made. But he had fine taste, and he introduced Mick to people like Phil Spector and Jack Nitzsche who had an important influence on some of the early musical efforts of Keith and Mick. And with his society-styled sense of the avant-garde, he shuffled just sufficiently ahead of the London Mod crowd to uncover some highly relevant effects just in time for mass

86

consumption: put-ons, pop epigrams, flamboyant tugs like the monumental Times Square billboard plus a corporate concept of packaging in which he wrapped the implacable uniqueness of Stones funkiness.

But Oldham was just passing through – even though it took him a number of years to drop over the vanishing point – and his relationship with Mick, in particular, was longer in the stage of decline than ascension. 'There were times,' Mick mutters, 'when we didn't even know if we had a producer or not. Sometimes Andrew would turn up, sometimes he wouldn't.'

'There was a time,' Keith admits, 'when Mick and I got on really well with Andrew.' Those were the days when Oldham stumbled upon Anthony Burgess' teen-age debacle *A Clockwork Orange* – a 50s-oriented street-classic which perfectly consummated the Loogian view of the fictional universe. 'We went through the whole *Clockwork Orange* thing,' Keith says. 'We went through that whole trip together. Very sort of butch number. Ridin' around with that mad criminal chauffeur of his!'

This butch number carried them through a series of successful outrages: promotional attacks upon abandoned baby carriages, much-publicised raised third-fingers, sombre pantomimes in which Brian tugged on an imaginary reefer while Keith characteristically showed his teeth and Mick replayed himself with a couple of quick-camps. Meanwhile Oldham slouched along with 'the group parents love to hate', scrutinising the events from behind his perpetual shades.

Together with Easton, Oldham arranged for the Stones' first record session at Olympic Studios. 'Look,' Andy said plainly, 'the difficulty is that this is the first recording session I've ever handled. I don't know anything at all about music, but I'm sure I know the right sort of sound which might prove commercial. Let's just play it by ear and try not to get too panicky about it all. Let's also remember that we've got the studio for three hours – and that it's all costing money.'

They dragged in their equipment and closed the door: the six Stones, Oldham and recording engineer Roger Savage. The result of the session was a disastrous version of Chuck Berry's 'Come On'.

The good folks at Decca listened to the take and didn't smile. They suggested the use of their own studios for a retake of the same tune. It was also a disaster. But after some effort Mick laid in his imperfect drawl and the boys laid down a 'bluesy, commercial' sound which, according to *Record Mirror* 'should make the charts in a smallish way'.

Mick was not happy on 8 June 1963, when 'Come On' was released. Recording was an experience he was entirely unprepared for ... a vacuum in which excitement was devoured by the dead air and unresounding walls. Without an audience Jagger could not get the atmosphere going. And all the success he had drummed up in Richmond seemed unimportant if that special Stones sound couldn't find its way on to a phonograph record. Besides, the Beatles' 'From Me to You' was sailing up the charts like crazy, leaving Mick dangling in fiftieth place. It was not exactly the soaring, sudden success he had fantasised for the Stones. The accolades from the music press. The smiles at home. The cheap thrill of hearing your voice coming at you from the BBC and the pirate stations! The frown of enemies – oh, so *many* enemies! And a glum look and resounding silence in the world of London jazz!

But it wasn't like that.

No, it wasn't how Mick had planned it. No instant pudding – with everything finally falling into place after the long hassle and the slow climb to the first recording and first TV appearance. Instead, it looked like there was always another hill.

But Oldham didn't let it get to him. He seized upon the small ripple caused by the release of the first Stones single and routed the press like a madman. A few dutiful reporters with nothing better to do called upon vocalist Jagger, curious to know if his hair-style was an imitation of the high-flying and booming Liverpool quartet. Mick was never one not to mince his words: 'Art students,' he exclaimed with his hands on his narrow hips and his woolly, woolly sweater sagging over his gesticulating shoulders, 'have had *this* sort of hair-cut for *yearssss* – even when the Beatles were still using hair cream!'

Later that year the Stones showed up at the National Jazz Festival in Richmond where they already had a solid audience. And in September they went on their first tour as the bottom act on a bill including Little Richard, Fats Domino and the Everly Brothers. 'On stage!' Mick exclaimed. 'I mean, we'll just go mad! Go *completely* wild!' He knew that his most important aim was to offset the soft-core impression. 'Come On' was making on the record market. 'If people don't like us, well that's too bad. We're not thinking of changing, thank you very much! We've been the way we are for much too long to think of kowtowing to fanciful folk who think we should start *tarting* ourselves up with mohair suits and short haircuts!'[1]

The crusade continued. The enemies multiplied. The jazz élite felt more justified than ever in its contempt for Jagger as pop disc-jockeys joined the rolls of Stone detractors. And yet at all the clubs they played the tables were filled to capacity, and the chickies were beginning to go fundamental-ape for Brian who had worked out these gestures which seemed to absolutely knock the girls out.

Mick noticed Brian's antics with mixed emotions. He felt pretty poor. He was rapidly fading into the background on stage as the chicks screamed at Brian. And he was being accused by enemies of being a hack imitation of Bo Diddley. No, it wasn't the way Mick had envisioned it back in Dartford. So he went silently back to the flat to soak up more R and B and to stand before his mirror where he commenced to fabricate with infinite care and imagination the theatrical style which would eventually make him into a superstar.

[1] Rolling Stones.

AS YOU MAKE PROCRUSTES' BED, SO YOU MUST SKIN-DEEP IN IT!

Michael Jagger, an intensely agreeable, self-contained, polite and rather quiet young man, has left the London School of Economics to take up permanent residency in his mirror. The Poet of Cocteau's *Blood of a Poet* plunges into his looking-glass, but Jagger resists that profoundly humorous posture of the artist-narcissist. He will not simply become immersed in himself, instead he'll use the mirror as a palette.

Sitting on the toilet in the darkness of the cold hall while his musical roommates sleep, Mick grunts and groans as he tries to find the voice of a separate race and a separate nation. Trying to turn his body inside out, like a magician's change-bag which always reveals the most improbable things when it is turned right again.

Or back before his mirror, drifting in and out of reflections. A penumbra. A virtual image like a rainbow which for all its marvellous insanity is really not there.

Mick stands like a photographer scanning the illegible shadows of a negative in search of light . . . that intangible shape of motion.

'What is that there?' Mick Jagger asks.

It is, like the mind and soul and inspiration, the disembodied fiction of bodily organs. Brain. Heart. And endocrine glands. It is a *mien* – something without proof or plasma. A quality which sets someone apart from all other people.

That's what Jagger was trying to find in the darkness of the toilet and the lumination of his mirror. A Frankensteinian metamorphosis: this fully grown plasmic pastiche with an adult brain full of nothing. To become something new. First through imitation and then assimilation and neurological ingestion. To devour a sensibility and in eating it to become it. A primal ceremony. A kind of complicated cultural cannibalism.

'Not Fade Away', released in February, 1964 brings a rough clooning of Ellas McDaniel/Bo Diddley into Mick's mirror. It's a reflection with a long afterimage.

Now Mick stands next to Brian and they sing a duet on 'Route 66'. It's not what Jagger had seen in his mirror. So with 'I Just Want to Make Love to You' he stands alone at the microphone and reaches down and finds the frail beginnings of a marvellous low voice, the bull-dyke voice which will become a permanent part of his artillery. The hard vowel-sounds start coming through with that characteristic *luuuuuuuuuve ta ya* enunciation.

'I mean,' Jagger explains, 'I don't think the lyrics are that important. I remember when I was very young, this is *very* serious, I read an article by Fats Domino which has really influenced me. He said: *you should never sing the lyrics out very clearly*. I don't try to make them so obscure that nobody can understand but on the other hand I don't try not to. I just do it as it comes. And I certainly don't want to go on stage and just stand there like Scott Walker and be ever so pretentious. I can't hardly sing, y'know what I mean? I'm no Tom Jones and I couldn't give a fuck. The whole thing is a performance of a very basic nature, it's exciting and that's what it should be.'

Back in front of his mirror, Mick unbuttons his pants. Dr John Money is standing in the wings with his book *Man and Woman, Boy and Girl* fastened temporarily to his brain.

In October of 1963, Dr Money explains impatiently, *a young rural couple took their identical twin boys to a physician to be circumcised. During the first operation, performed with an electric cauterising needle, a surge of current burned off the baby's penis. Desperate for a way to cope with this tragedy, the parents took the advice of a sex expert: 'Bring the baby up as a girl.' The experiment has succeeded. With the use of plastic surgery and with upbringing as a daughter, the once-normal baby boy has grown into a nine-year-old child who is psychologically, at least, a girl.*

In his mirror, the imitation which Mick, like all males, accomplishes first is masculinity: that chain of events, beginning with the choice of a male name, that determines that the child will behave in traditionally masculine ways. On the song 'Honest I Do' Mick gives us his impersonation of respectable 1950-Pick-Up-Truck mentality. Next on 'Now I've Got A Witness' a Stones original, Mick blows fair harp. 'Little by Little' is still locker room-Jagger, butching it up and doing a back-seat quickie with the action centred on the band. 'Togeeether we could make honey the woooorld has nev'r seen!' Mick niggerising with a fake, greasy dialect and a very heavy debt to Bo on 'I'm A King Bee'.

But Jagger was not a black man. And he gradually gave up the delta fantasy. There would be some true imitators . . . marvellous, uncanny imitators like Eric Burdon. But as for Mick Jagger, he was looking for himself among the black wailing bodies in the galley of the slave ship. He didn't want to be a one-man minstrel show.

And Jagger didn't want to be John Wayne either. So he gradually gave up the butch act. What he was looking for was the kind of ambiguous sexuality which drifts through the pages of D. H. Lawrence and Jean Genet.

Meanwhile he records 'Tell Me' – it sounds like Sha-Na-Na on a good night with just a few touches of the ballad style of 'Lady Jane'.

'Can I Get a Witness' is the ass-end of Mick's gospel romance. 'Walking the Dog' is painfully Anglo-Saxon: one of those insanely serious and literal approaches to *black camp* which the twenty-year-old English kid from Dartford doesn't yet understand.

Dr Money's twin boys, now altered into brother and sister, reappear in the mirror. For the little boy who lost his penis, the change began at seventeen months with a girl's name and frilly clothes. An operation to make the child's genitals look more feminine was done, and plans were made to build a vagina and administer estrogen at a later age. The parents, counselled by psycho-hormonal experts, began to treat the child as if he were in fact a girl. The effect of the parents' changed attitude towards the child were amazing. 'She doesn't like to be dirty,' the mother told the clinic. 'My son is quite different. I can't wash his face for anything. She seems to be daintier. Maybe it's because I encourage it.

She is very proud of herself when she puts on a new dress, and she just loves to have her hair set.'

Just prior to the beginning of 1965, the Rolling Stones *12 × 5* is released in America. The boys are still shirted and suited on the album's cover, and, somehow, Brian still seems most predominant. . . .

The Album begins with a good-natured rocker from Chuck Berry. 'Around and Around'. 'Confessin' the Blues' is more interesting for its piano licks than its vocal. But then with 'Empty Heart' Mick flickers into focus for the first time: the phrasing on the bridge is the first uncertain stage in a transmigration. But the alteration is very gradual: Jagger still has the unmistakable air of a college grad on a Saturday night. Flat-faced and blank and shy.

In 1890 Eugène Henri Paul Gauguin packed up everything but his astonished family and took off for Tahiti. He hatched from a businessman into a painter. But who knows what really happened and for how long the stress was building up in this immense nova . . . before the burst of light. Before the process became an appearance.

For Mick Jagger the progression was slower and less conscious. He thought he was on the stairway to heaven but he was actually going straight to hell. Like Rimbaud, Jagger proclaimed: '*I is another*.' And what enfolds during the next few years is a sublime and subliminal expression of a new humanism. *I contrived to purge my mind of all human hope.* Rimbaud said that at the age of nineteen.

> *On the black gallows, one-armed,*
> *Bland, they dance and dance, the paladins,*
> *Thin paladins, the devil's band,*
> *The skeletons of Saladins.*

Having spent his youth searching for goodness and having found none, Rimbaud attempts to sink to the lowest depths in hope that he might find the truth there. Mick Jagger was on the same trip of the mythic hero with a thousand faces: he signed off at 3 a.m. one dismal morning with the lyrics to 'Sway': *Did you ever wake up to find a day that broke up your mind . . . Can't stand the feelin' . . . gettin' so brought down.*

But in 1965 he was not aware that his transformation from a person to a personality would cost him his life. He did not foresee the terrible cycle which would see the record business kill music and then the record industry kill itself, turning everything into the science of packaging and marketing. Jagger did not foresee his transformation from musician to rock's first entertainer. He meandered gradually into the seventies. Retaining his elegance and funkiness in a perverse balance. Waltzing into the Degenerate Follies, a musical freak show replay of Berlin of the 1930s. The era of Josephine Baker's tits and Marlene Dietrich's vaguely transvestite mannerisms. Opening night of *Wozzeck* and *The Threepenny Opera* – the marriage of Freud and Karl Marx. The Berlin nightclubs where the bizarre became chic: Nazis in bustles and lip-rouge; whores in military drag. The quintessence of finely-tuned anal art. Men with painted lips, glittered faces, high heels and a capacity to outrage which makes Broadway's *Cabaret* seem a bit like *Snow White.*

The public found in this marvellous perversity a sort of Wagnerian edition of *True Confessions* and *Screw* thrown into one. That's of course, what Bowie and Bolan and Cooper are all about: they allow a whole bunch of heterosexuals to get into psychological drag. Part of the musical chairs which makes copy for the various cash-and-carry underground rags has to do with proving regularly that they are *truly* decadent. Mismatching their biological and biographical facts, intermingling their ladies and gentlemen in print but rarely in bed despite all the rumours. And lifting Jagger to the sky in fashion and society columns. *Hosanna Hey Sanna Sanna Sanna Ho! Hey MJ, MJ won't you smile at me? Sanna Ho Sanna Hey Superstar!*

Goethe provides Mick with his epitaph: *I had to give up my life in order to be.* But spoken Bette Davis-style: *I had to giffup! my life in aaawdah TO BE!*

And Mick Jagger epitomises the romance of dilettante

discomfort: *Headin' for the overload, Stranded on a dirty road; Kick me like you kicked before; I can't even feel the pain no more.*

The first Stones classic is 'Time Is On My Side', a tune by Norman Meade, on which Mick does some very original phrasing as well as a perfected blackface recitative. But the message is improbable.

The Jagger-Richard original 'Good Times, Bad Times' also isn't much. But there is now an indication that if Mick is ever going to get it on it's going to be on tunes authored by the Stones themselves in which the vocal line fits Jagger's formative style.

'Under the Boardwalk' is just summer-stuff, hot dogs and french fries. But the original 'Growin' Up Wrong' is the first authentic Jagger-sound . . . it's unmistakably ministrel show Diddley, but it also begins to possess something unique to Mick.

'Satisfaction' is up in the top ten and *The Rolling Stones Now* is one of the biggest albums of the year.

Mick Jagger steps up to the microphone as Tina Turner to record 'Everybody Needs Somebody to Love'. It's rumble-seat darkie music, with a touch of Amos and Andy on the introduction. The flamboyance surfaces slowly, the bitchy pout resounding in the phrasing. But the vision is still antebellum plantation. 'Down Home Girl' comes off like black bubblegum: '*I kin tell bah yur giant steps, youv bin waaalkin' thru a coooton fiiiild!*'

Keith and Mick collaborate for the most impressive original to date: 'Heart of Stone', the second Stones classic.

'Little Red Rooster' is dead-pan literalism which misses the barnyard black comedy of Memphis by several thousand light-years.

In the middle of 1965 the Stones return for a second bout: *Out of Our Heads* . . . the boisterous replay of tapes made in Hollywood, Chicago and London. In no other album can the theatrical transmigration of Mick Jagger be more clearly heard.

'The Last Time' introduces the characteristic nasal tone which Mick was building into a style. And the song ends with the first fully developed crescendo, with Jagger's shouts anticipating the mini-opera he will eventually deliver with 'Goin' Home'.

'Play with Fire' is an exceptionally controlled version of this song with the lyrics and tune way up front. 'I'm All Right' is the first *live* Jagger madness on record – giving us some grasp of the holocaust out front as Mick joyously shouts 'All right! All right!' at the end of the tune. The good Reverend Jagger: '*All right!*'

In 'The Spider and the Fly' there's the classic line 'She said she liked the way I held the microphone' ... the emergence of Stones autobiography-in-song.

And, of course, there's the absolute all-time rock tune 'Satisfaction'.

It's an extraordinary song, one which rises out of its era and expresses many varieties of experience on many levels of mentality. It's the perfect Stones paradox – the words turn around and deny what the music communicates. 'Satisfaction' was at least five years ahead of its time and yet it completely dominated the summer of 1965. Parents agreed with the frustrated redundancy of the tune as they banked their small paychecks and paid their large bills. Kids shouted out the chorus when they were confronted with the strictures of school days. And older brothers and sisters gleaned that perhaps one verse of the song was about a girl who won't put out because she's having her period. 'Satisfaction' had something for everybody; and yet it's far more of a revolutionary anthem than 'Street Fighting Man' insofar as it conveys the universal frustration of a people endlessly faced with institutions and destiny and nature. But there is irony in the song as well, like so many Stones tunes which take on the ills of society; the fact that Mick Jagger is singing about frustration is just a bit of a twit.

'December's Children' closed 1965. It offered something

new in the Jagger-Richard cosmos: 'As Tears Go By', the first step towards the ballad style of 'Lady Jane' after the earlier and less lyrical 'Tell Me.' Richard combined with Mike Leander on an unheard-of moment of string arrangement on a Stones cut.

'Get Off Of My Cloud' is pure Jagger, without effort or postures. 'Route 66' reappears in a version hardly changed from the original recording except, of course, for the insane crowd. The phrasing is a bit more sophisticated and there is more stress on diction than in the prior version.

'Talkin' About You' is perhaps the most conspicuous song in terms of showing where Mick is headed; with its gospel grunts and outcries, it's clear that ecstasy is near.

The first Golden Age of the Stones commenced in 1966 with a US collection of their *Big Hits* (*High Tide and Green Grass*). About the same time the Mike Nichols filmic version of *Who's Afraid of Virginia Woolf?* breaks down cinema censorship and unleashes the tide of subsequent porn. Bishop James Pike begins the Ecclesiastic Demolition Derby when he breaks with the Church and goes spiritualist. 'Ballad of the Green Berets' is number one while *The Sound of Music* is the top-selling album in the States. Sinatra has got him a 'Stranger in the Night' which is more quizzical than anyone imagines, and the wise men offer these pronouncements:

FK: 'In such a fantastic and dangerous world, we will not find answers in old dogmas, by repeating outworn slogans, or fighting on ancient battlegrounds against fading enemies long after the real struggle has moved on. We ourselves must change to master Change. We must rethink all our old ideas and beliefs before they capture and destroy us. . . . America must look to its young people, the children of this time of change. And we look especially to that privileged minority of educated men who are the students of America.'

Wall Street Journal: 'It was hard enough to tell the boys from the girls anyway, what with hair styles and perfumes and everything. And now comes this new fashion trend. It's enough to make a parent lose his cool.'

Then came the album *Aftermath*

The first classic collection. Everything seems to fall into place. The country stuff on 'High and Dry' has real character. The harp, the bottleneck guitar ... the chugga-chugga bottom ... it finally sounds like an authentic musical style. And, of course, 'Going Home' is the 11:35 minute transworld express! With 'Paint It Black', 'Stupid Girl', 'Lady Jane', 'Doncha Bother Me', 'Think', and 'It's Not Easy' among the best of all possible worlds.

Got LIVE If You Want It! brings it all together. Fully orchestrated with the hysterical audiences of 1966. The recording and performance techniques have merged. 'Under My Thumb' is almost a full minute faster than the previous version. 'I've Been Loving You Too Long' is a second-hand rose, but on it Mick does more very high vocal work than ever before ... likes it and adds it to the charisma which he now holds solidly between his legs.

Jagger: 'Sometimes we run things down ... sometimes we get an idea for a song from say a rhythm that Charlie and Keith have played together or something. Quite often, we go into it without the song being written ... which annoys me intensely. But, that's the way we record sometimes. I like it to be rehearsed before we go in, but it never really happens. The music quite often comes ahead of the words. That also annoys me. It's very hard to write lyrics to the finished track. It's much easier to have it done before but . . . .

'I always try to write the lyrics to the songs. Like that thing with strings on *Moonlight Mile*, the lyrics weren't written to that before we cut the track. That was very extemporised. We didn't *think* of having strings or anything. It just comes.'

Jagger is the literary personality. Keith handles the music. But Jagger also has a very strong impact on the shape and theatrical form of the songs. Jagger is a very great musician but a rather mediocre composer.

The First Golden Era closes with a set of three albums in 1967: the most important year in the phenomenon which will probably be called the Children's Crusades of the 1960s. *Between the Buttons* opened the year with the singularly most brilliant collection of tunes created by Jagger, Richard and the Stones to date. A set of hits follows in the album *Flowers;* while the tribute to the era of mind and mould is *Their Satanic Majesties Request.*

With 'Something Happened To Me Yesterday' Mick did his very accurate Bob Dylan impersonation and ends with a parody on the trad Saturday hop: 'If you're on a bike, wear white!' Most of the other tunes on *Between the Buttons* experiment with instrumentation with a high degree of success: the unique om-pah bass on 'Complicated', the strings on 'Yesterday's Papers'. Ragtime piano and sitar on 'Cool, Calm and Collected'. The pastoral thrust of 'Ruby Tuesday', and of course the flagrant innocence of 'Let's Spend the Night Together'.

1967 ushers in the transplanted heart and the off-Broadway portrait of hippiedom called 'Hair' which the high priests of the scene mark for failure. *Gentlemen's Quarterly* decides that 'Mod is dead'. Marshall McLuhan predicts 'an economic depression within about five years'. Dr Spock tells us that 'The enemy is Lyndon Johnson.' Bonnie and Clyde introduce the Outlaw Look. Jim Morrison sings 'Light My Fire'. And Sgt Pepper slowly ascends into the stratosphere where the Monkees are trying to be friendly with Jefferson Airplane.

The Stones will re-emerge with *Beggar's Banquet, Let It Bleed* and *Sticky Fingers,* but the Second Golden Era will be a corporate act and not the individual strivings of the members of the band to establish a public personality. The Mick Jagger of 'Sympathy For The Devil' and 'Street Fighting Man' is a consummate professional, trying his hand at theatrical revolution. Brilliantly Brechtian: inflammatory, accusing and utterly vague. The Jagger of 'Midnight Rambler' and 'Brown Sugar' is a sophisticated stylist, trying his hand at Madison Avenue Sadomasochism. Brutal and afflicting, but it's all bottled blood. And none of the close calls are really very close.

Mick smiles contentedly. The long march is over at last, and he rides the crest with the nervous relaxation of a superstar. But even from the room at the top you cannot see the future. Just ahead is the morning of 12 February 1967, when he is arrested on a drug charge and will become, like Oscar Wilde, the centre of a tide of public resentment. Also ahead is the death of Brian Jones in a swimming pool, and the death of a nonmovement at the high altar of Altamont.

West 23rd Street isn't much. It's got a series of grey pizza parlours, a couple of over-priced deli's, and the inevitable Horn and Hardart. There are a few flower shops where flowerless old men sit all afternoon. There's a Spanish café and a Steak and Brew and an oyster joint where you can get the most outrageously impolite service in the western hemisphere.

It's not much. But ever since they started calling it *Chelsea*, these expatriated uptown types have been buying up the old brownstones and remodelling them for a large fortune. The old neighbourhood is changing. The PRs have made their trail of tears in the general direction of Yonkers, leaving only miniscule traces of their long boardinghouse residency in the area: legions of cockroaches, a couple of bars where they still sing songs about *Me Corazon*!!! and a few shops where they sell platanos and hundreds of bent cans of Goya brand pimientos. *Olay!*

Unfalteringly, the Berny 'Y' squats in a brown funk in the middle of the block . . . staring across the street at no. 222: THE CHELSEA HOTEL whose big neon sign progressively spells less and less.

'*T-E -HE-S-A HO--L*' is an 1882 apartment-hotel which has housed many of America's distinguished and drunken authors. Thomas Wolfe among them. Gertrude Stein. Dylan Thomas. Composer Virgil Thomson walks its dim halls. So have Ragni and Rado and Viva. Occasionally a supergroup in the mood to slum settles into one of the terrifying green rooms with its single 150-watt incandescent glowering from ceiling.

It's New York's highest priced slum. But it's got what they call *cachet*.

Rita's waiting in the laboured lobby . . . crammed with *objets d'arts* and vending machines. He's obviously nervous, constantly closing his navy pea coat over his crushed velvet skirt. The desk clerk who has seen *everything*, including the face of God and the Jefferson Airplane's dirty dishes, glances at Rita and picks his nose. Rita's wearing his really colossal silver and green Joan Crawford-Fuck-Me-Shoes. Ankle-straps, platform soles . . . the works! The clerk gives his crossed skinny legs a once-over. 'Ya waitin' on somebody, honey?' he nudges.

'Ya,' Rita says shyly. He self-consciously closes his coat over his bony knees and ignores the old guy.

'You an actress, honey?' the desk clerk persists.

Rita laughs an Anne *All About Eve* Baxter laugh and says: '*ahummmm*. . . .'

'Thought I recognised ya. I kin al'ays spot ah entertaina, ya know. Ever time!' And he laughs his Richard *Kiss of Death* Widmark laugh and Bogey's on the counter while he gives Rita his big Peter Lorre eyes.

Rita reaches into the repertory and pulls out his Veronica Lake big frost. The desk clerk sullenly goes back to sorting mail. And Rita goes back to worrying about the Stones party and birthday concert. *I'll die . . . lord, I'll just die.*

When I walk into the Chelsea Hotel and introduce myself to Rita, the old man at the desk gives me a dirty look. But the grimace is so customary in New York that I ignore it and sit across from Rita. I begin by chatting aimlessly, trying to get him to relax and talk about himself. But Rita is intensely shy. He keeps gazing at me suspiciously.

I'm not the kind of person he had expected . . . he confides to me later . . . hardly the nice family doctor/journalist from *Our Town* to whom he can comfortably reveal his heart of hearts.

'Tell me, Rita,' I smile, using a bit of male guile, 'would

you object to telling me your real name? I mean, it would probably be interesting to people. . . .'

'No, no,' Rita says very seriously in a voice which is uncustomarily masculine. As if he feels like he's got to play it straight for the press despite his outrageous wardrobe.

'So, what is it?' I ask.

Rita smiles. '*Harold Schartzberg*,' he says flatly. And then he leans towards me and whispers: 'Isn't that *horrible*. . . . I mean, how *anybody* could life with *sucha* name!'

I've been trying to get an interview with Harold Schartzberg for two months, ever since seeing his incredible performance in a hit underground film. Getting the phone number from the producer was easy, but getting Rita on the telephone was something else again. I called every day. Either there was no answer or a polite young lady would answer and explain that Rita's not home. 'Yes, I gave her your messages, but she's really tied up with a film right now. Y'know, rehearsals. . . .'

'Do you think you'll be seeing . . . ah . . . him soon?'

'Well, sure, I'm her *temporary* roommate, y'know, and I see her, like, all the time.'

'Well, do you think you could explain that I called again and that what I want is an interview with . . . ah . . . Rita?'

'Sure. . . . I'll tell her.'

Now Rita shrugs his shoulders: 'So I'm not goin' to live with that kind of a name . . .' he says, giving the desk clerk a dirty look.

'I think,' I say with a bit of bravado, 'that the transformation is marvellous.'

He is obviously pleased, and for the first time releases the coat he's been clutching closed, and pushes his flat veloured chest into the Chelsea light-of-day. '*Wait* till you see what I have to do in this *new* movie that I'm doin'. . . . I mean, it's *simply wanton!* I love it!' And he laughs. 'It's so fabulous, y'know, the way people treat me now.' And he rolls his eyes and extends his hand to an imaginary admirer for a kiss. 'Just terrific,' he whispers, glancing at the desk clerk and giving me an Eve Arden frown. 'Like, my God, at Bloomingdale's today. . . . I mean, the *whole* place was just, y'know, packed around me . . . all the other counters complained . . . and they were putting all these cosmetics on me. It was a Mary Quant counter . . . so now, they're givin' me free make-up! *Mary Quant*, I mean, my dear, that's *class* . . .' and he glances into the mirrored hall and mumbles, '. . . all these colours in my eyes. . . . y'know. . . . like, I don't know how to use the liners properly. . . .'

'It looks fine,' I say. 'Really nice.'

Rita gives me her extra-wide Rita Hayworth smile.

'What is this I hear about your playing a boy in your next film,' I ask.

'Well, ya, there's a scene where I go to a party and I fall in love with myself . . . y'know, like, what do they call it . . . a dual-role type of thing, y'know. I play both a girl and a boy. And the girl falls in love with the boy.'

'But your major role in the film will be a girl, right?'

'Right . . . like, she comes to New York to become a *star* . . . and she goes through a series of, y'know, bummers. She meets all kinds of weird people . . . who are, y'know, *sicker* than she is.' And he giggles. 'A midget who lifts weights . . . a bearded lady who suffers from penis envy . . . a sword-swallower whose girlfriend is a kleptomaniac . . . that kind of thing. *Very* sick.

I ask what Rita did before he started in films.

'I was in an off-off-Broadway play . . . y'know . . . with the Theatre of the Ridiculous . . . you know what that is? It's like the Cockettes only it's so *much superior*, my dear. I mean, the Cockettes, how should I say, are just acid-heads in drag. There isn't a *star* among them. Not one! But the Theatre of the Ridiculous was sublime! I mean, really, *sublime!*' And he whispers: 'Y'know, *very* high class and arty and half-the-time-I-didn't-even-understand-what-the-hell-I-was-doin'!' And Harold Schartzberg bursts out laughing and wipes his nose on his sleeve.

'Jackie Curtis has done some work with the Theatre of the Ridiculous. . . .'

'O, sure! In fact, she wrote this play I was in! I was a

103

chorus girl, y'know. *Oooo*, I was *so sick* ... I *loved* it!' Rita Mae-Wests emphatically.

'And were you discovered?' I ask.

'My God, *certainly* I was discovered!'

'Tell me how . . . .'

'Well,' Rita says with heavy Ethel Mermanese, both hands commencing an elaborate Semitic choreography, 'my current producers, y'know, came to see the production! Well, they spotted me *immediately!* I mean, *really!* So one night I'm in Max's and Fred Ross comes over and asked me if I wanted to be in a movie. . . . *I'm gunna say no?* So that's when I did that flick. . . .'

'Did you have any idea it was going to be such a big hit?' I ask.

'Course not ... but, after a while ... like, when I saw the whole thing at screenings ... and everybody started telling me how good I was, y'know. But I never imagined it would go *that* far! It opened in Atlanta Christmas Day! *Can you imagine!* Those queens down there are still screamin'! I'm getting fan letters from Ohio and Illinois. ... That's how I met my boyfriend ... he saw the picture in Puerto Rico! I mean, are you ready for a mail-order bride!'

'Do you feel like a star?'

Rita smirks and then makes a long purring sound: '*Yaaaaaaaaaa!* Why not!' and he gets very dreamy for a moment and tries to focus on the excitement of being a celebrity.

'It's fun to have people run up to you in the street ... but,' he complains, looking into the mirrored walls, 'I wish I didn't look so kvetchie ... but, I mean, who says that you *have* to be *glamorous!* Shit! I'm not just a pretty girl ... I mean, let's face it. But I have a hell of a good time!'

I see an opening and quickly step in: 'Is that true?' I ask softly. 'I mean, do people really allow you to have a good time, Rita?'

It's a direct hit. Rita gets misty.

'Well, y'know, I have to tell ya,' she murmurs, 'that sometimes it ain't exactly a pleasure. Y'know I'm not just a queen in drag. I mean, like, I've got feelings. When I'm out of New York, y'know, people have *no* idea. I mean, they wouldn't know where to begin. . . . As far as they're concerned, I'm a girl. And they're so *friendly*. Really, it's amazing how friendly they are. *Just people*, y'know, I really love them.'

'When did you get into . . . permanent drag?'

'It was nine years ago . . . I ran away from home in San Bernardino when I was fifteen. . . . All I took was this *schmottah* I wore Halloween. And I drifted around. I didn't have any money . . . I didn't have any luggage. But there are queens *everywhere*, my dear, like an underground railroad . . . so I just went from one sister to another . . . lookin' for god knows what. Y'see, I love fantasy. Y'know, I always loved a good fancy-dress movie. So I wanted to be a *star* . . . always . . . I always wanted to be a *star*. Y'know on film you can live out *any* fantasy. Like, I've always wanted to be a mermaid . . . y'know. So I'm sure that one day somebody's gonna come along with a script where . . . like, they need a fuckin' mermaid! So, I'm the one! But I don't think I could hold my breath under water that long . . . y'know . . . I'd have to have a gay stand-in for the underwater parts!' And he laughs and loosens his coat over his shoulders, executing a quick Monroe-puckered-pout.

'Did you drop out of school?'

'School? . . . can you imagine *me* in high school in San Bernardino, my dear. Can you believe *San Bernardino, California!* I mean, I was totally demented. *De-mented!* The high school hoodlums used to protect me . . . like, I used to be their mascot . . . that was my only salvation . . . otherwise, I'm tellin' you, they would have *killed* me. And the teachas . . . oh, my dear, the teachas were appalled. Cause all I could ever think about was Mick Jagger. Day and night I used to dream about Mick. . . . I just loved that bitch! She was always such a fuckin' camp and *nobody* could shut her up! Like I remember the first U.S. tour. We went crazy . . . all of us. They were coming to San Bernardino! My God in Heaven! Can you believe how it felt to be visited by the

Stones in *San Bernardino, California.* It was like Judy Garland doing *A Star Is Born* IN PERSON, that's what it was like! Jesus, I remember I got the albums and I played them until they were worn out. And ... that's right! ... they played the 'Hollywood Palace'! You remember! You remember that TV show? And that sonuvabitch Dean Martin ... that lousy wino wop! I mean that SOB, he had the nerve on *national* television to say the things he said! *Their hair,* he said, *is not that long ... it's just smaller foreheads and higher eyebrows.* Can you believe your ears! I mean that was 1964, and these people thought that if you were a little bit different from them that you deserved to be ridiculed! I mean, to put people down like that! Like they didn't have any feelings. That Dean Martin! *Actually,* he said, *the boys are soon back to England to have a hair-pulling contest with the Beatles.* Can you believe that bastard? And what's *he* so fuckin' proud of, anyway: some elephants and chorus girls dressed up like Western gun-slingers? The King Sisters? Is that what's so fuckin' civilised about the 'Hollywood Palace'! ... But the Stones, y'know, the Stones, my dear, are not ones to be messed with. I'll tell you ... they gave a press conference on a traffic island outside the *Chicago Tribune* offices on North Michigan Avenue. The fans went mad. Everybody showed up for that! And Charlie Watts, my god, he's so *marvellous!* This girl, do you remember reading about it?' Rita cries, clasping his hands and laughing. ... 'This fan, she ran up to Charlie and asked for a souvenir ... and Charlie offered her a *chair!*' Rita roars.

'But Mick,' Rita says, 'Mick is the one. I mean, she's so heavy. She's just plain outasite, my dear. All that shit they hand her, always trying to bring her down, y'know ... and then there was that poll which shook everybody up. Cliff Richard got first place as best-dressed pop artist ... but lurking down there in sixth place was Jagger! It was a stone gas! Everything she did was like that ... I remember following all of it ... year after year. I was such a fan. ...' And Rita smiles nostalgically. 'Dah-ya remembah Chrissie, Jean Shrimpton's little sistah? Well, she and Mick got it together

... mar-vel-lous ... it really was marvellous. Then at Swing Auditorium, San Bernardino, there must have been ... maybe five thousand kids there! I never seen so many kids before ... it was like a fucking-football-game, that's what it was like! The police couldn't keep the chicks down. Jagger almost got dragged off stage. You couldn't even hear *Not Fade Away!* It was the big American hit, y'know, so we all went completely mad. And *Mick! Oh, Mick!* I had never seen anybody like him before! Not ever! It was everything I had ever dreamed of ... y'know ... the whole universe and everything! And as I watched him and heard everybody, the girls and the boys and everybody screaming, well, I knew right there that what I wanted to be was a real *star!* A real *star!*' And Rita gives me his Margaret O'Brien!

'Mick, y'know, he's such a demented one. The way he carries on is simply outrageous ... and *I love it!* Then in 1965, remember, he started seeing Marianne Faithfull and everything. I remember that cause like I kept a scrapbook for maybe three years. Everything about Mick ... *everything!* All the girls at high school! ... we watched for clippings and pictures. We even got the Stones fan magazine! Then there was Bianca ... a real Carmen Miranda chick! Dietrich and Miranda, what a trip! Cloche! Feathers! And, my dear, that cigarette holder ... an absolute fruit-fly. A regular Bette Midler, my dear ... a girl imitating a boy imitating a girl! Quite a switch, dontcha think from butch ole Mother Courage ... Marianne. I mean, my dear, do you know that she was devastated ... really devastated ... when Mick gave her the slip. Sister Cocaine, *indeed!* Poor thing was hospitalised, I hear, put on the boobie express and hasn't been the same ever since! Such a tragedy ... really a *tra-ged-ie.*

'But I never thought she was really right for Mick, y'know. . . . She never seemed like the right kind of chick. . . . I mean, my dear, who needs an armoured-guard for a girlfriend. Not even Oscar Wilde needed that kind of cover ... and Bianca, well, what can I tell ya ... she's a party favourite ... that's all she is ... one pop and she's had it!'

And Rita laughs. 'But Mick has known so fuckin' many people! I know more girls who have tried it . . . and God knows how much you can really believe of what most of them tell you. . . . I know how I talk on an up and a glass of Ripple!

'There's a chick right here in this hotel, y'know. A marvellous chick! Well, she met Mick. I mean, she met Mick when he was just a baby. She's a photographer, y'know, and she had this show in L.A. With Lichtenstein and Warhol . . . when they were just starting to get a reputation, y'know. A few freaks maybe know about them. Well, she had a couple of these painted photographs in this gallery in L.A. and Mick was there on the '64 tour, y'know, and being a very artsy sort of guy, he went down to this gallery to take a look-see. And he toppled over this chick's painted photographs. So the way she tells it, she got an invitation to go to the concert – where was it? – in Oakland? Was it the *Fox Theatre* in Oakland? Well . . . anyways, she trucked her ass up there hoping for the best. I don't really know if he screwed her or not . . . like I said, you can't count on most of what you hear . . . but she's got some incredible photographs of him. Jesus, so innocent and cute and nice! And he took some films of her with this old 8mm camera that she always uses. And she took some films of him . . . nude . . . with an erection. . . . It's supposed to be *really beautiful*. But that was a long time ago, and who knows. . . .'

Rita is very quiet for a long time. It's getting dark out on West Twenty-third Street. And the desk clerk is puffing in his sleep.

'It must be lovely,' Rita says softly, 'to be a real girl.'

'Why don't you take a trip to Sweden or somewhere? . . .' I murmur, getting caught up in the enormous alienation of Harold Schartzberg.

Rita looks up with astonishment. Then he laughs a dry laugh. 'I don't want to be a girl,' he says flatly. 'There are boys who would like to be girls and there are boys who would like to be boys pretending to be girls and then there are boys pretending to be men. Now it seems to me that you can be absolutely any of these boys without wanting to have sex with other boys. What makes you people always assume that a guy in drag is a girl in a boy's body!' And he looks annoyed. 'Doesn't it ever occur to anybody that I could be happy *just* the way I am? Sex doesn't have anything to do with sexuality! That's the most obvious thing in the world! I mean, I've known *that* since I was fifteen-years-old in San Bernardino, California!' And she gives me her disapproving Crawford eyes, and pulls her coat over her shoulders. 'So what's the matter with all the rest of you!'

As Altamount gradually comes over the horizon (recapitulating a perfect Yeatsian nightmare) it becomes clear that Woodstock and all that it signified about the sixties has been a wet-dream.

'And what rough beast,' Yeats asked, 'its hour come round at last, slouches towards Bethlehem to be born?'

Mick Jagger knew the answer. Hadn't he written the lyrics which go: I sung my song to Mr Jitters, Yeah, And he said one word to me, And that was 'death'?

But obviously Mick didn't see this premonition as the come-down it would become at Altamount — anymore than student militants grasped the potential horror show of their rebellion until the murders of Kent State and the explosion of the house on West Eleventh Street.

Jagger confused Genet's vision of the gangster as saint with the American dream which imagines the gangster as poet. That's why the team of Jagger-Richard has such a strange resemblance to the Brecht-Weill collaboration. Both Brecht and Jagger express a very similar political innocence: an inclination to forgive brutes as losers, to heroise the working class and at the same time to abhor political aggressors. The premise of imagination upon which Brecht and Jagger envisioned America — each in his vastly dissimilar way — is not simply a matter of getting the facts wrong but of developing a credible falsehood. After all, Puccini had Italianised Japan in Madame Butterfly *and had melodramatically envisioned 'a vast desert on the borders of New Orleans' in the last act of* Manon

Lescaut. *But these are mere 'anthropocentricities' – not conceptual inventions.*

Jagger insists upon a paradox. He dreams about the exiles on Main Street, but he also toasts the 'salt of the earth' with very mixed emotions: 'They don't look real to me, In fact they look so strange. . . .'

Jagger inherited the principal hallucination of talented fops like Tennessee Williams and Jean Cocteau who transformed their sexual idols into poetic truck drivers. The image is false and brutal and negative. Part of the Franco-American inclination to heroise bandits, killers and soldiers. A fetish which has a very complex sexual life in the masturbatory fantasies of the prior generations.

The concept of the bandit poet is an easy theatrical device. It motivated a hit film like Bonnie and Clyde *– the transformation of truly homicidal narcissists into tragic heroes! It kept a perverse and trendy attitude towards the Hell's Angels alive for a number of years. And it justified a whole lot of uniform fetishists, from Kenneth Anger to Yukio Mishima.*

But if this vision of the hoodlum as poet is a vastly influential falsehood based essentially on the homosexual temperament, the importance of homosexuality to pop culture is also quite undeniable. Camp, put-ons, and a special kind of grotesque self-mockery are indispensable elements of the basic sensibility of pop. These are not the only elements which pop culture taps from a secret reservoir. The relationship between the two largest underground minorities and pop is so fundamental that it's been all but overlooked. Most of the language, look, ilk and image of pop comes from the worlds of blacks and homosexuals. These underworlds have been the richest sources of contemporary imagery . . . and so it's only natural that Mick Jagger should be closely identified with characteristics borrowed from both identities.

Keith takes a careful look at Mick. 'What's wrong?' he asks.

Mick ignored the question and took a deep breath before he opened the dressing room door. Outside the kids had formed long, frenetic lines on each side of the hallways which tunnelled the Los Angeles Sports Arena. The bulls were doing their best to hold them in check, but the screams were like a strong wind blowing in Mick's face.

He closed the door. 'I think I'll sit down for a minute before I go out,' he muttered.

Everybody looked at each other and it got very quiet in the dressing room all the sudden. Keith glanced at everybody and sat down beside Mick, lowering his head next to his and mumbling nothing in particular as he lit Mick's cigarette.

'There's no big hurry,' he laughed awkwardly. 'We've done the last concert for this tour and we can damn well afford to relax a little.'

The first tour of the States in 1964 was not what Mick had hoped it would be. He stood up and walked towards the door. Obviously he wanted to get off by himself. Everybody made their way through the crowd. Mick got very quiet in the limousine. He just put his head back and closed his eyes. No, it had not been what he had hoped it would be. . . .

David smiles wearily when I balance my way past him, trying to get to the buffet while there's still some food. The hefty chick who is dangling her feet in his stoned pop-speak is a young editor from one of those perilous paperback houses which hired house-hippies back in 1967 to serve as youth-experts-and-interpreters and have never quite figured out how to get rid of them now that the senior editors themselves have learned how to speak 'Hippie'.

There are lots of editors at the party. It's a New York party. 'Love-ly place you have here,' somebody I don't know simpers as she passes, giving me that *choke on it* smile. Like I said, it's a New York party. So there are lots of editors, actors, agents, models and boyfriends. The grass isn't very good and there's booze in the punch. Jackie Curtis is on the balcony imitating Karen Black and Karen is downstairs imitating Sylvia Sidney. Only she doesn't know it.

It's a New York party.

A well-known poet reads *The New York Times* while his

drunken boyfriend lights a succession of matches and holds them dangerously long between his big fingers. The leading lady currently at the Alvin sits with a chorus-boy who keeps telling her this everlasting bit of gossip.

People keep arriving: early in the evening most of the arrivals are friends or friends of friends, but as the evening marches on, the faces become more and more remote, until 3 a.m., when it becomes pretty apparent that the arrivals are strangers looking to get turned on and fed.

A little pack of dancers whine incessantly, scrambling into chairs; while the poet looks up impatiently from the *Times*. A tall slender blonde makes his magnificent way between the guests escorted by two bodybuilders from the Coast. The leading lady has passed out and her winsome friends has joined the dancers in their perpetual jabberwocky. Three underground film-makers, eyes weary from the evening's Movieola-ing, smell sour as they walk past. And groupies with wild crowns of hair and big painted eyes. And the disc-jockey from Danny's Disco. The model on last month's *Vogue*. The girl who takes hats at the Schubert. Two Bejart dancers. The secretary of an advertising executive with her frail girlish friend. And Sammy Schwartz who just recently got out of jail.

David is starting to get the look of a man about to make excuses and say *Good night*. I'm just about to attempt to cheer him up when one of *Esquire*'s brightest flashbulbs arrives with a small mob. 'Hope you don't mind if I brought a couple of friends,' he says as this whole fucking regiment troops in.

When I attempt to introduce David, the Esquireen with the parade leans over and whispers in a modified shout: 'David who? Oh . . . heavens, now I know: he's one of those *underground* writers.'

David is either stupendously innocent or fantastically confident, because he's untouched by the bullshit. He wanders back out into the crowd. The record producer who put together the last Joplin album and got a hit for Jake Holmes smiles at me.

'O that guy,' hisses a small-time journalist with hair bristling from his nostrils, 'he's a fake. *Everybody* knows that!'

Musicians who are entirely strung out on everything simultaneously. Guys who gave up loving music three years ago in an RCA recording studio, but keep playing. And guys who so utterly love the notes which they themselves play that their every utterance is music. They call it jazz. Managers who go through people's careers like fat ladies picking out just the chocolate-covered cherries in a five-pound box of candies. And agents whose belief in your genius lasts forever till it dies. Attorneys who know confidential things about *everybody* . . . which they expound very privately in loud voices. And revolutionary FM personalities who sulk in faded jean-bundled wrath. They sit glaring at the people wearing colours and explain to the guys sitting next to them how they really aren't part of *this* crowd.

In the middle, a spacious clutch of dancing-fools have abandoned themselves to the roaring music, semi-nude, semi-mad and semaphore.

'You know what F. Scott Fitzgerald said, don't you?' David mutters as I flop down beside him on a couch.

'No,' I say, 'I don't know what F. Scott Fitzgerald said.'

'He said that everybody's youth is a dream, a form of chemical madness.'

'Oh my god,' I mutter. 'I really don't believe that I'm sitting here wasting this inordinately fine head on this conversation!' David just smiles. He's had a beef with his old lady and I know that he's thinking something like: *And you think you have troubles!*

'OK, David,' I say, '. . . let's have it. What's on your mind?'

David grins through his perfect midwestern disguise. 'How's the book coming?' he asks.

'Slowly . . . very slowly.' And he looks at me. '. . . because I find it very rough,' I explain compulsively, 'to explain the duality of somebody like Jagger. I mean, he's so quiet. He's so basically refined and polite. And yet's he's got this marvellous cunning and keenness. A sort of animal thing dressed up like a middle-class Englishman.'

'Why don't we get out of here for a while?' David says, leading me towards the door.

'Jagger,' I say, as we wander down Fourth Street towards Sixth Avenue where David can get a Howard Johnson's ice cream cone, 'he's a monumental lover. He's not only the magician with a mysterious song in his throat and a cock visible in his pants, he's also the satanic wonder who stands in for all the totems and taboos which we're intent upon wrecking. You know what Laing says . . . we're the colonists, and in order to sustain our amazing images of ourselves as God's gift to the vast majority of the starving human species, we have to *interiorise* our violence upon ourselves and our children and to employ the rhetoric of morality to describe this process. Our parents do it and we call them cannibals. But we do it ourselves . . . we just employ a different vocabulary to sustain our images of ourselves. *We are effectively destroying ourselves with violence masquerading as love.* Jagger is that kind of lover. But unlike the ones we go through in a hurry: *wham, bang, thank you, Ma'am.* The affair with Jagger keeps going. He's got staying power. We can't quite grasp the parasexual shadow he flaunts. It embarrasses us even to talk about it.

'The kid who tells his girlfriend that he'd like to ball Jagger receives her enthusiastic agreement. It's just one more thing they have in common. And while Taylor and Cocker sink back into the pillow and want to go to sleep, we roll over and lie there thinking about our next musical lay. Our next hot romance! Cocker or one of the other burned-out stars may sulk and try to make another flash – but it's improbable that we'll care very much even if they do manage to get it up again. Once you've had somebody, you've had them.

'But Jagger – well, he's something else. He's Lola Montes. He changes the course of history. He's Isadora twisting old man Singer around her finger. Callas methodically destroying Rudolph Bing. Sarah Bernhardt! One of the miracle-people. We simply can't love them to death. So they keep on living. That's what a myth is ... something we can't destroy through comprehension.'

'Hey, tell me something,' David inquires as we pass the barred and boarded façade of what used to be The Sanctuary back in the days of rock 'n' roll, 'what is your professional opinion of Howard Johnson's ice cream?'

I ignore him. 'But,' I say sternly, 'what makes us recognise these myths? What makes us need them?'

'Now *that's* fucking incredible,' David melodramatises. 'Go ahead, tell me!'

'OK ... I'll tell you!' I shout over the heads of the various creatures from darkest Brooklyn who line the counter at Howard Johnson's. 'It's because we've been totally devaluated.'

'What?'

'I said: *devaluated!*' I shout, as a cluster of people sweep between us.

'You jes' watch who yah shoutin' at, mistah!' the girl next to me admonishes. I try to ignore her and edge my way through the crowd towards David just as he gets two scoops of chocolate ripple on a sugar cone. 'Everything is crumbling,' I tell him as he sucks up. 'Ya know, we are the hollow men sorta thing. The absolute self-righteousness of America is gone. I mean, that went with the U-2 spy thing. Or the Pentagon Papers or the My-Lai mess or the Watergate Affair. You name it. ... And *our* leaders – I mean the ones *we* mystify – well, either they get assassinated or we find out that they helped get us into this mess to begin with. And the church – well, you know about the church. And the occult. . . it turned out to be a novelty shop once we came down.'

'That's true,' he mumbles between licks.

'Is that good?' I ask.

'Want a bite?'

'No ... and that doesn't leave us very much. I mean when we ask ourselves what we believe in it doesn't leave much.' And I watch him licking the cone as we turn into newly sanitised Washington Square. 'Well, as all of these things were collapsing around us, we needed and we desperately wanted the only reasonable confirmation imaginable: some kind of *deep, passionate experience!* Y'know what I mean: *sensation beyond the ordinary*. Now that kind of experience and the burning need for it wasn't invented by this generation. I know all about that ... so don't interrupt.'

Now it's reached the hour when it's late even for New York. There's nobody left to stare at. Nobody left to bump into. Or to yell ethnic remarks at. No one to suspect of imminent violence. Nobody ... but a kid in this lone, lighted telephone booth, desperately trying to get his last dime back from the violated change-box.

'After all,' I say, stepping over an old guy who's passed out on the pavement, 'the romantic poets were after the same thing. We're the same kind of rebels. Insistent upon having a *real* experience. Even daring madness in order to discover it. Ingesting potions that do god-knows-what to our brains. Searching into all the dark corners and looking for the ultimate madman who will dare more than we are willing to dare. And that's where Mick Jagger comes in.'

David and I are silent as we turn back towards the party, arriving to find people crashed everywhere and one fantastically twisted guy still dancing in the nude in the middle of the void. The stylus hissing out the last endless circular groove of an LP.

'Like most profoundly stimulating social forces, Mick Jagger evokes far more than he means, suggests more than he is, impels conscience beyond his scope, ideas beyond his intellect, visions beyond his imagination. That's the basis, of course, of his majesty. He is more than he is.

'He's a puzzlement. Offering the most glittering female impersonations in the world outside a good English public school where it's been a strange English custom for centuries for boys to heighten camp to the status of revelation. The English have a thing about this and you can't really begin to understand Mick until you understand the relationship between camp and self-mockery and the strange English sense of humour.

'But, of course, it doesn't end there. Mick's too smart to make public poses without having a vengeance behind his behaviour. He's questioning lots of things – consciously and semiconsciously. The classic clinical interest of male psychologists in the origins of homosexuality. He's questioning the premise that a *terrible experience* is the only possible basis for the sexual behaviour of so many *thousands* of people. In other words, he's posing the question which revolutionary lesbians have been asking: what he wants to know is how people get to be heterosexual.

'Jagger's trans-sexuality is just one of the things which makes him qualify as our great hero. He's always two-faced. He's a male chauvinist who acts like a fop. We know that logic won't work, so we figure that maybe illogic is where it's at. He writes outrageous lyrics about dumb girls and then he turns around and acts like one. He says something about unconditional armed revolution and then asks us *what can he do but sing in a rock 'n' roll band*. He's the only rocker with real old-fashion star-quality and yet he infuses it with so much self-mockery that we see him as an anti-celebrity celebrity. And the Stones always came on looking terrible. They were dressing like hoodlums when other groups looked like Pat Boone. And they sang about drugs and took pictures with naked ladies and motorcycles. They wore leather jackets and gave the world the finger. And yet, there was always Jagger, carrying on like some kind of tart. At the same time he sang to us about the male's principle preoccupation: getting into a girl.

'Jagger inherited the Brando mystique. But he also accepted a dowry from Marilyn. Let's face it, Mick is a male impersonator. And I'm not talking about standard, Eisenhower, bull-dyke masculinity, like John Wayne or somebody. I'm talking about Brando and Dean and Garfield and Newman . . . guys who played at being guys. A rather beautiful boyishness well concealed beneath a heavy coat of industrial paint. A glimmer of narcissism as touchy as wet paint.

'Exaggeration is part of this kind of stylisation . . . it wouldn't work without it. And Mick's career is largely indebted to the capacity of the middle-class to detest anyone who departs from their narrow vision of social reality. *Jagger is it!* He's to Ziegfeld what Alice Cooper is to vaudeville. He's the temple harlot. Keeping the sacred fires of hermaphroditic dieties. The mother superior of David Bowie and the legions of camp stars who are steadily becoming the new trip. It's all part of his duality.

'What he does with this series of contradictions is present them with the kind of energy and irreverence which touches off the *myth of ourselves*. He delivers. A tremendous wallop! Even the disbelievers can't stay out from under its influence if they're at a performance of his powers. Jagger seems to dare anything! He steps out on the most perilous thin coating which supports our sanity. He ignites the terrible violence within us . . . a violence compounded of our desire for *something* . . . *anything* with real magnitude. We want our lives confirmed. We want to *feel* what it is to be alive. The life we are trying to grasp is the us that is trying to grasp it. Sartre said, *You are your life and nothing more*.'

David sat among the passed out people and stared at me for a long time. The nude guy was still undulating in slow motion, reaching upward for a sign of himself. Then David sighed. 'And tell me, how are you going to get that kind of thing into a book?'

'I'm not sure.'

And he lit a joint and passed it slowly, nodding and watching the dancing figure. 'I mean,' he said, 'how can you set yourself up to tell people what people are thinking?'

I didn't answer.

'I mean, what kind of shape can a book like that have?'

'Well,' I said, feeling a little stoned again and sailing off, 'I imagine it will have to be something like an orchestration . . . y'know, like Berio's *Sinfonia* . . . a collection of quotations and bits and pieces from everywhere.'

'But is that the truth? Is that kind of thing really the truth?'

'I don't know what the truth is,' I said. '. . . but it will be true. Everything in it will be true.'

'And don't you think,' he asked, 'that perhaps people might object to the fact that you had *this* particular conversation with somebody else. I mean, that events which may have been singular have become composite. And that you've injected into things not the emotion which exists *in* them but the emotion which you feel *towards* them?'

I smile and say: 'David, it's like Jill Johnston said: *I thought all the stories I read were marvellous inventions. I knew I could never do it myself. I couldn't imagine people and events that weren't my life. I didn't know that fiction and reality were in reality the same.* You see, in nonfiction we tell about real people and use real names and in fiction we tell about real people and use fake names.'

'Well,' David said, 'that's all very well and fine, y'know, but people have this notion about facts.'

'But David,' I tell him, 'you miss the point! I'm telling you this because I urgently want the book to be *real*. But it *is* a book. That's part of the reality. And I wouldn't want my honesty to make people think I'm dishonest.'

'Well, if I were you, I wouldn't say anything about it in the book.'

'I won't,' I say.

He stared at me for a long time. The sun was turning the windows grey. Suddenly you could smell all the sleeping bodies and the stale glasses and filled ashtrays. David got up and stretched and walked to the window. 'It's another terrible day,' he said.

'Yes,' I said. 'Do you want an up?'

Dominique hadn't slept well. The roar of the trucks had kept him up all night . . . tossing around in his sleeping bag and counting the bleak spattering of stars which bleed faintly through the overcast. Through the fumes of carbon monoxide.

It had been a mistake to camp along the highway, but the trip up from San Diego had been so gruelling that he never would have made it into Frisco. So he rolled his motorcycle a few yards off the highway just south of Redwood City, where he threw his sleeping bag on the weeds and immediately crashed.

It was almost 6 a.m. when he cried out in his sleep and sat up, peering anxiously down the dew and monoxide-filled freeway. Taking a moment to realise where he is and what he is doing there. *My god*, he mutters. Altamont is still thirty miles away and he'll never get *near* the stage if he doesn't get there before they open the gates!

So he shakes his head and brushes off his rumpled clothes. Gotta make it to that historic get-together! *Altamont, Jesus!* And a rush hits him ... he doesn't know why. He gets wowed by this swimming feeling. Partly because he's a little ... what do you call it? ... well, maybe like *worried*. Cause, y'know, he hasn't really hung out in these scenes much. Alan always talked about it, sure, but actually they hadn't been to but maybe four or five concerts in Dago and another couple of littlish events in La Jolla.

So Dominique wasn't exactly certain what had compelled him to roar all the way up just to see the Stones. Of course, it was the big thing to do. Everybody in Dago was talking about it. Shit, that's all you heard lately. *The Stones! The Stones!* And it reminded him of the way Alan used to talk. Y'know ... before Alan got messed up. Before he got wiped out. ...

Of course, Dominique had read all about Woodstock. He even got the album and special issue of *Life* magazine with all the pictures and everything. Well, actually Alan had gotten the album, but they both listened to it for hours ... for weeks they listened to it ... till it seemed to them that they knew every word of every tune and every announcement and the thunder of the applause and the sky and the rain and the wind and the chanting: *No rain, no rain no rain, no rain, no rain, no rain, no rain, no rain, no rain, no rain, no rain* ... until it was like they had been there too. In the mud and having a

ball and stoned out of their minds! *Sure, man, it was great!*
It was – like – the high point of my life! And everybody on the
beach would be so fuckin' impressed ... looking at Alan
and him. Really impressed! The chicks too ... *Alan said*
that the chicks really got knocked out when him and me talked about
Woodstock!

Soon the traffic was backed up ... maybe ten miles. Kids
hanging out of buses and smiling ... and horns honking
like it was New Year's Eve. Nothing could get through that jam
except maybe a bike; so Dominique meandered between the
cars and vans and campers, while people tossed him crazy
comments.

Finally he pulled into automotive Nazareth. Nothing like
what he had expected ... just miles of unfinished freeway
which were doubling as the world's largest parking lot. He
chains up his bike and starts over the miles of asphalt. Not
knowing exactly where he's going. Just following the huge
rank and file of dead-end kids.

'... if I see that sonofabitch I'm gonna cut his throat,
man, and I'm gonna break his legs!' this guy is saying when
he walks past these ratty-looking boys who are lugging a
big pack and a wheel off a bicycle. Nobody is smiling as
they march into the cloud of dust that's blowing off the dirt
embankments surrounding the perpetual asphalt gangway.
Nobody's smiling and nobody knows where the road ends.

'Look, Murray, you said we wouldn't have to walk ...
so where the hell is it, anyways!' this chick is hissing at a
disgruntled guy. But Dominique's mood is good. Despite
the slow trodding tribe ... glum and irritable. People pump
on joints and dip into wine bottles, but their spirits are
pushed out of shape by the congestion. *Californians don't like*
to be crowded, y'know. It's not our thing to be crammed.

It's a long march. Past a strange old beatnik type dressed
up like god-knows-what. He's maybe fifty years old ...
dead-white and whiskered. With a scattered patch of long
hairs on his head and loads of dime-store necklaces around
his neck. Rings. And this green satin Shakespearian outfit
with a cape and everything. He can't walk very well and

he's stumbling along the shoulder of the road, stopping every few minutes to catch his breath. Everybody ignores him.

Further along there's a tall, skinny chick taking off her clothes while her boyfriend is drawing something on her back with a lipstick. And in a small whirlwind of dust there's an old man working in iron. He looks up at Dominique and smiles and then disappears in the cloud. *What!* Dominique cries out, feeling a rush and spinning around to find the old man. But he's gone.

The faded blue people behind Dominique trudge dead-pan around him as he stands there staring after the spectre. They don't see him. Nor do they see the pilgrim sitting cross-legged on the road. Squatting in their midst. A sphinx-child: immobile except for his perpetual, mad grin. Alternately he flashes the V-sign to the troops with both his hands, then suddenly he gives them all the finger. First one. Then the other. Repeatedly.

Dominique slowly raises his hand to his mouth.

At seven o'clock they open the gates. Over the hill and down into the clearing by the platform comes this oceanic mob. In minutes the locusts have denuded the meadow and bodies are pressed into a wad. But the crowd keeps coming over the hill and by ten it has seethed outward unwillingly ... a quarter mile back from the stage.

And when I search a faceless crowd, a swirling mass of grey and black and white, they don't look real to me; in fact they look so strange, Mick sings under his breath in one of the dressing rooms at the Tarant County Auditorium, home of the Miss Teen-age America Contest, where the Stones are getting ready to scintillate Texas. 'Very pleased to meet you, excuse me, not now, later ...' Mick says automatically. An embarrassed silence. Somebody comes to the rescue, tucking a cassette into a machine. WHERE CAN I GET MY COCK SUCKED? WHERE CAN I GET MY ASS FUCKED? WHAT'S ... somebody quickly interrupts Mick's recorded message. 'Wrong cassette,' he grins, and slips an alternative into place. Now music accompanies the assorted, sorted remarks.

Mick has vanished. And the remaining ensemble is rather downcast. The afternoon concert had been a responsible replay. Now the huge auditorium has been re-stocked. It is 102 in Fort Worth. A characteristic brutality has followed the Stones down from Chicago and Kansas. The heat ... and the wave of resentment which lays upon the calidity worries Mick a little. The South has a reputation for ferocity, and each step along the tour could be another disaster. And, lord knows, they don't need another disaster!

The 1969 tour wrecked a lot of heads. It had the stench of greed and blood. Resentment and recrimination. Everybody was talking about *Charles Manson*. The only good thing that happened to the Stones that year was the fact that Manson decided to play 'Helter Skelter' to his old lady instead of 'Sympathy for the Devil'. But everything else was a bummer. The Maysles Brothers' film, *Gimme Shelter*, was supposed to celebrate the Stones' beneficence and an unbounded western bloom of Woodstock beatitude. Instead it recorded a Californian *Götterdämmerung*. Incriminating everyone in sight until someone made a hurried transcontinental phone call which revised the film's final version to stress Jagger's intense sorrow over the whole bloody mess.

Now it was 1972 and the Stones arrived in what seemed to be a less violent America until the attempted assassination of Wallace and the paranoia which followed. The tour was moving as inconspicuously through the States as an elephant stampeding down Main Street, Omaha, Nebraska. But so far everything was pretty cool. 'I tell you, that Vancouver shindig almost put an end to the whole thing,' an official-looking member of the Stones' pilgrimage murmurs under his breath. 'But we've learned how to do it.' By the summer of 1972, in Fort Worth, Texas, the Stones are doing a vaudeville act, surrounded by the largest batallion of hired cops since Golda Meir got an unsolicited copy of *The Arabian Nights* in the mail. Mick is looking forward to the fabled

Deep South which has rumoured through so many of his lyrics. And, of course, there's the big birthday concert which is planned for New York, America's sole-city!

The tour has become a literary congress. Writers are sending home stories about other writers. Truman Capote boarded *The Tongue* in Kansas City and has been looking annoyed ever since. Tequilla Sunrise is flowing as the flip trip of this elder congregation of bored journalists who have come fully researched in the native language and appropriately transvestmented and dressed-down. As has been their wont since 1969–70 when it became smart to look weird. To the common people out front it looks a bit like Cleopatra's barge.

'What happened, my dear, is that they got their asses busted, that's what happened!' Rita shouts to his friend Brenda Starr who is so twisted on downs that he is only millimeters away from unconsciousness. Rita continues to pace back and forth while Brenda slowly bats his enormously lashed eyes and mumbles with just his lower lip. 'The press, the fucking shopkeepers, the queens, the stars ... I mean fucking everybody just loathed them. I mean, my dear, they were like pregnant nuns!' Rita exclaims, addressing himself only partially to dozing Miss Starr, while he also conducts a sort of universally directed lecture, with all the appropriate hand gestures and pauses for reaction. It's as if he is practicing a speech.

He pauses every now and again and glances at the telephone. 'Where is that muther!' he mutters. 'He's supposed to call *right* back!' And he takes up his frantic pacing once again. '... anyway, supposedly *The News of the World* planted somebody or tipped somebody or something. But Jagger had this slander suit going against the paper, y'see, and so they decide to shut him up *good!* How d'ya like that bullshit, huh! I mean in a democracy and everything! I mean, my dear, even when you're a *star!* I mean, *really!* how rude!' Brenda Starr laughs his way back into a bit of consciousness and Rita hugs him and rolls with laughter. 'Are you ready for that?' Rita roars. '. . . even when you get to be a fuckin' *star* they won't leave ya alone!' Then he lowered his voice and got a very bridge-game-seriousness: 'I knew one of the chicks at the party . . . *personally* I knew this chick. Nineteen policemen showed up. At eight o'clock Sunday evening there comes this big knock-knock at the door of Keith Richard's house, my dear! *His* house! *Well*, who is inside when Sgt Cudmore hands Keith the warrant? I'll tell you who: Mick Jagger! Robert Frazer, a girl, a Moroccan servant and a few friends!'

'. . . yayayayayaameeeeeeeeean,' Brenda blows as if he's deflating, 'yamean . . . they get . . . ahhhhhh . . . busted?'

'Naturally there *had* to be a dealer there! Just their luck, y'know. And he's carrying enough to fix up everybody on a good night at the *trucks*, my dear!'

The phone rings and Rita lunges for it. 'HELLO! . . . O, I thought maybe it was Jackie . . . no, I'm just waiting to hear from her about something . . . something *very* important. No, Brenda's here, honey, just wait a minute and I'll take the phone over to Sleeping Beauty and you can tell her yourself . . .' And he hands Brenda the phone. 'What a *nothing, a complete nothing* that queen is,' Rita mutters when Brenda stirs into conversation. 'Your friends, Miss Brenda, are such evil faggots, my dear, I just can't tell ya! Who the fuck does she think she's comin' on with! . . . that fucking tea-room size-queen. The nerve! That faggots' mouth is bigger than her ass . . . and, believe me, that's going some!' Rita pauses just long enough to look out the window to see if Jackie's coming. Brenda Starr drones on, unmoved by Rita's diatribe. But Rita isn't finished. '. . . so tell that cunt to get off the fuckin' phone in case Jackie is trying to call!' And he returns to keep watch at the window.

There is a collection of freaks. Jesus-look-alikes by the dozens. Smiling, dirty babies. Gorgeous and not-so-gorgeous topless girls. *And the crazies.*

125

There seem to be more and more crazies at each festival. Lots of speed freaks, of course; dazed and hastily lined with age as if by a branding iron, missing teeth and constantly on the very edge of a stupendous rage. Blank-faced acid heads, burned out by too many flashes and too many collisions into the barrier of consciousness. Hare Krishna people, dogmatically chanting about the one and only god to unwilling passersby. Guys in leather jackets with the kind of girls who used to clutch a guy's side and grimace at the world like a mean kangaroo from its mother's pouch. And guys with conceited grins and beer. Boogie and bravado.

There are a couple of shaggy numbers leaning on their bikes. Filthy hair hanging down from their motorcycle caps. Stringy beards. A black man is bouncing in the middle of a small applauding crowd. It's the first concert where there are lots of black people. There are more girls than usual, too . . . probably almost as many girls as guys.

With the girls have come a lot of guys yelling: 'Hey, man, you keep lookin' at me chick like dah and I'm gonna break ya back!' Most of the smiling college students intent upon making the world into a French landscape painting have vanished. So have the tow-heads from Iowa who used to walk around in a blaze of astonishment. Smiling. Pacified by potions, pot and panaceas. Riding on a surge of humanness. And music. Surcease of alienation. A truce . . . temporarily.

A cowboy type strolls against the current of people with a card stuck in his hat: ACID $2.

Michael Lydon looks around and says: *Face by face, body by body, the crowd is recognisable, comprehensible. As ugly beautiful mass, it is bewilderingly unfamiliar – a timeless lake of humanity climbing together through the first swirling, buzzing, euphoric-demonic hours of acid. Is this Bosch or Cecil B. DeMille; biblical, medieval, or millennial? Are we lost or found? Are we WE, and if we are, who are we?*

One-third of a million post-war boom babies gathered in a Demolition Derby junkyard by a California freeway to get stoned and listen to rock 'n' roll – is that what it has all been about?

Woodstock was a three-day encampment at which co-operation was necessary for survival; it was an event only because it became an event. The Altamont crowd is DEMANDING that an event come to pass, be delivered, in a single day!

Richard Elman looks around Forth Worth as the Stones charge on stage and says: 'The constantly made analogy to Albert Speer's Nuremberg rallies of the thirties is accurate in one sense; it's not so much a question of ideology as of stagecraft, of somehow seeming to be leading an avant-garde for millions; yet, there are, sometimes, moments when ideology and stagecraft seem to be but different facets of the same glittery gimmick.'

Meanwhile Jagger is leaping into the air and tossing rose petals everywhere, and the overhead mirrors slowly pan into the audience and flash bursts of light upon the hysterical crowd. Mick says THANK YOU! And everybody hurries into the camper which is waiting outside. The doors slam shut and they roar away – racing silently over thirty miles of freeway to the Hyatt House in Dallas.

Backstage in Houston it's another opening, another tantrum. Keith roars in shouting: 'That Stevie's a bloody cunt!!!! He just called Mick from Dallas. He won't be here this afternoon, and maybe not this evening either! It's his drummer . . . had a nervous breakdown!'

Mick flies in and whirls around several times, attacking the metal lockers and making a lot of noise. 'That *Stevie*,' he hisses. 'That bastard! Expects *me* to believe that shit . . .!'

'You know . . .' Keith mutters, 'they probably had them a big night . . . you know . . .' And then he shouts: 'FUCK THAT CUNT . . . HE'S A CUNT!' Mick grabs hold of him, embracing him quietly for a moment, whispering something. Looks around at the astonished press and friends and hangers-on. Tour manager Peter Rudge makes an entrance like a Cambridge headmaster. The silence is preposterous.

'If he doesn't make it tonight,' Mick murmurs flatly, 'he's finished. He's through . . . no more jive. . . .'

'. . . fuckin' Stevie. . . .'

'Come on, band,' Mick mutters slowly, looking around uncomfortably. '. . . not here . . . let's get it together . . . this way, please. . . .' And they retreat into another room.

'How do you like that!' whispers a journalist with a little granny face peeking out from behind his pampered locks. 'Can you just imagine such shit! If Stevie Wonder can pull a thing like that. . . . I mean, it's nonsense. What does he want – a star on his dressing room door? Who the fuck does he think he is, anyway! So what if he can't fly in the plane, so bloody what! There wasn't even enough room for the *Princess*, I mean . . . not even for Truman's *best* friends . . . so, tell me, what does Stevie want! *What does he want!* So what's so terrible about using the bus they gave him? Oh, come on, what troubles? He can get places to stay and places to have a good meal, man, this isn't the fucking Civil War, y'know. So it's the Deep South, so what? Are you trying to tell me that Stevie is afraid of the South, man, is that what you're tryin' to tell me.'

The Houston concert is a smash despite the hassles.

But Rita is in a terrible mood. It's already getting dark and still there's no word about tickets for the concert! Nothing. . . . 'Anyway, the Stones got busted! But what could they pin on them, I ask ya?' Rita is saying. 'Mick has a couple of amphetamines he bought across the counter, I mean legal and all, in Italy. And they get Keith for permitting people to smoke shit in his house, y'know. Big deal, huh!' And Brenda Starr slowly nods out. Rita lunges at him and shakes him until his gigantic lashes unseal. 'Honey,' Rita shouts, 'what's the fuckin' point of getting stoned if you're gonna fall asleep and not enjoy it! Come on, Brenda, you fuckin' pig, wake up and keep your ugly little eyes open or I'll slap your face silly. . . .'

'Wha . . . wha . . . ah . . .' Brenda stutters weakly.

'Are you awake? . . . can you hear me? Well, just stay awake, god-damn you, 'cause I'm not sitting here by myself tonight! Waiting . . .'

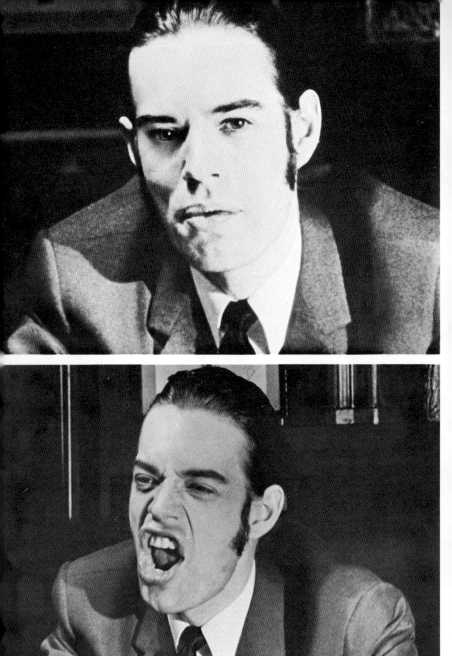

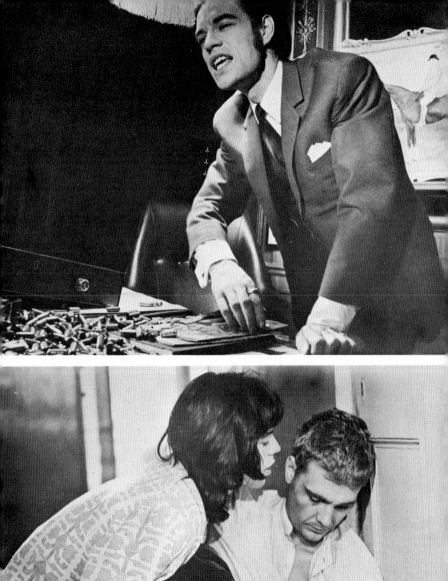
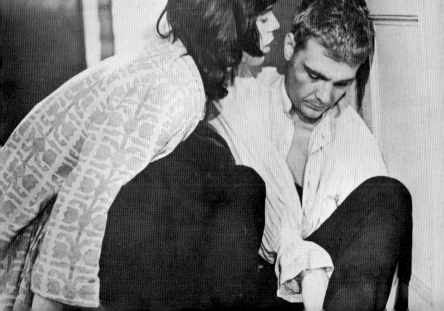

'Wah . . . wha . . . ah . . .' Brenda is stuttering.

'Anyway, where was I? . . . Oh ya, well, they were just gliding down from a twelve-hour trip, y'know. Mick's first, if you can dig it. And in comes the fuzz! My God. . . . I'd die a thousand deaths, my dear, a *thousand deaths!* Weeeeel . . . Brenda! . . . Are you listenin! . . . weeeeel, out on gay bail, my dear, Mick and Keith slink off to Morocco to wait it out till the trial. And what a trial it was! . . . here, I want you to open those ugly little red eyes of yours and look at this scrapbook, Brenda. Brenda! . . . right, look at this, I mean *really*, even the London *Times* was on Mick's side!'

THE LONDON TIMES: LEAD EDITORIAL
1 JUNE 1967

Who Breaks A Butterfly On A Wheel? It would be wrong to speculate on the judge's reasons, which we do not know. It is, however, possible to consider the public reaction. There are many who take a primitive view of the matter. They consider that Mr Jagger has 'got what was coming to him'. They resent the anarchic quality of the Rolling Stones' performances, dislike their songs, dislike their influence on teenagers and broadly suspect them of decadence, a word used by Miss Monica Furlong in the *Daily Mail*. . . . If we are going to make any case a symbol of the conflict between the sound traditional values of Britain and the new hedonism, then we must be sure that the sound traditional values include those of tolerance and equity.

'Well, by the end of 1967, Mick was the crowned prince of darkness as far as England was concerned. He was rich. In fact, he was *very* rich. He was a star! A *Superstar!* And he carried on in public like a fucking fruit.'

But the masked loathing of this flagrant young man was far more bitter than anyone imagined. Jagger was a cultural assassin. There were people who loathed him who had never even met him or heard him sing. Just because he challenged the status quo.

What refined people want is security – their comfort demands that things remain as they are. Whom they fear and therefore most loathe are those who by insinuation – rather than by direct action – threaten the enriching calm of history. Jagger was a calamity to them because his threat was perfectly ambiguous: not what he himself enacted so much as what he stimulated in the actions of others. He and his Stones were an affront on every level: as educated men, as musicians, as *Englishmen*.

Jagger's multiple insinuation deeply offended London's purism and pride, a reaction which could be duplicated in only one other city: San Francisco. London and San Francisco both have a chic fetish for antiquity: cable cars, plaster edifices, lawns and institutions. They blush at the excesses of their sister-cities: Holywood and Paris. They like to note that they keep their wealth behind closed doors and not on display. 'One has to discover London gradually,' they like to intone eloquently. For them art is largely regarded as that which has already been accomplished. And excess: loudness or vigour, imagination and flamboyance are not polite.

But it was not these people who tried to decapitate Mick Jagger. It was the press, the most questionable vehicle of the mass media which balances its morality somewhere between H. L. Mencken and William Randolph Hearst.

So the folks at home had nothing good to say for Mick, and the press had a perpetual hard-on for anybody who successfully challenged their appointment of greatness, and – worst of all – there were the other bands who loudly loathed the unbending, kinky contagion of the Stones. In a fiercely competitive business like music, Jagger was the perfect target for sore losers who attacked him personally in retaliation for his professional success. There is, after all, nothing worse that you can do a fellow musician than succeed!

As for the press, it was sick to death of the Stones. Columnists had been prodded and cajoled for years to give space to a band which didn't play their kind of music. A band which was rather dirty and stupid-looking and one which flaunted certain very *unnatural* attitudes.

Jagger himself had been very properly ignored by the press. *After all, what could a person like that expect,* they whispered between pints at the Fleet Street pubs. Yet Mick had had the keen audacity to splash all over foreign headlines anyway! It further outraged Jagger's enemies when they noticed that the German papers often chided the London press for ignoring these superb creative musicians.

So with the manipulation of the highest of horrors, DRUGS, the ugly journalism moved in on Jagger, shooting him down with insinuations while all the time crying out in headlines for Truth! People who had never interviewed him picked up the notes of cub reporters and fabricated articles; re-enacting those forgeries so often written by critics who don't attend the performances they review. This was the ilk of journalism which poured into the newspapers.

For a while it seemed that no one would recognise the falseness and cruelty of the attacks on Jagger as a person. That no one would call a halt to the madness for just a moment in order to remind the scandal-loving public of the enormous achievements of the young man who was being attacked for so slight an impropriety that it would be regarded as an amusing behind-the-scenes story if anyone else had committed it. In order to suggest that perhaps the whole scandal was a self-conscious cover-up for a newspaper's blatant infraction upon ethics and a salve for journalists who felt just a bit guilty because they were not part of the Stones' ascension.

The London *Times,* unexpectedly, proved why it is still the greatest newspaper in the world by rationally coming to Jagger's defence. Anything else would have been shameful. But the incident reminds us that exceptional people are the mysterious provokers of rage. Mom and Dad were glad to see Jagger shamed. The hip musicians smirked and muttered about guys who get excessive with their extramusical shit,

and the press struck another blow for universal normalcy –
the enriching calm of history.

Only the London *Times* insisted upon reason.

LEAD EDITORIAL: 1 JUNE 1967

There must remain a suspicion in this case that Mr
Jagger received a more severe sentence than would
have been thought proper for any purely anonymous
young man.

'Soooooo,' Rita says, 'they gave Keith a year and they gave
Mick six months! Can you believe your ears, my dear! Can
you! Now, I mean, a *year!* Isn't that just too much! Those
fucking English hypocrites!'

'Wah . . . ah . . . y'knowwwwwww,' Brenda is muttering
slowly. '. . . Karl Marx, y'know, he said it was gonna be
the first capitalist country to go to the dogs. . . . I mean I
read that.' Miss Starr smiles weakly when Rita gives him a
look which mixes disbelief with contempt.

'Well, anyways,' Rita says, still staring at Brenda Starr
with mixed emotions, 'they threw the whole thing out of
court when they appealed it. I mean, *some people!*'

Dominique is pretty stoned by now. It's already noon and
there's no music yet. He looks around, trying to wade
through the people who fidget and undulate but don't go
anywhere. He can't see anything but people . . . magnetised
by a four-foot-high platform. So Dominique presses in that
direction . . . compelled to escape by the constant pressure
of all the bodies around him. Feeling like he's in the way
. . . like he's pinned down . . . struggling for air . . . space . . .
a margin of personal territory.

He's sweating nervously when he gets to the stage and
climbs on to it, seeking its relative openness. Nobody cares

. . . nobody seems to be in charge. So he stands there for a moment, in the clutter of equipment, photographers, very young chicks who look like they're on the site of the second coming, abrasive, pushy members of the crew and a few Hell's Angels who stand in clumps like black Rhinos at a tea party.

Dominique turns and looks back out over the crowd. It's endless, flooding into the distance and vibrating with a cold, impersonal rumble. The guy next to Dominique gives him a blank stare followed by a dirty look. Nobody's smiling anymore. They've come for the freebee *so just get out of the way, brother, and let me through*. Dominique ducks as they rush equipment past him.

'How come the Angels are here?' this skinny chick asks him, looking off into the distance. When he doesn't reply, she gives him a critical glance.

The microphone sputters suddenly and the crowd brays. But it's only the Stones manager, Sam Cutler, begging the people to make way for an equipment truck which can't get to the stage area. Nothing happens, so Sam repeats the request. There's no joy at Altamont. People groan and bitch and slowly get out of the way. Dozens of guys with nothing better to do but re-enact the 40s, hang off the hobbling truck for a dismal joyride and a ten-foot ego-trip.

Santana jiggaboos into action. The crowd isn't pleased. People keep talking and milling around. A couple of isolated types are getting off on the music, shaking their asses and spreading a bit of happiness to the mass immediately surrounding them. But the rest of the crowd chokes on the massive crush of themselves. The only hand-holding is being done by couples who are showing off their sexual trophies. Like kids at a prom.

Dominique feels lonely in the crowd of thousands. Isolated and snubbed. Ignored. Guys standing next to each other at the urinal, with that forced expression of privacy where there can be no privacy. Tempted to look down to see what the next guy has got, but incriminated by the notion and compelled instead into chummy conversation or abject silence. Looking dead ahead at the tiles. Moving a bit closer or farther from the wall, depending on how you're hung. Or how you've *fantasised* your equipment ever since the day you discovered that there's more athleticism inside the locker room than on the field. And all these chicks . . . an extension of that same frail game. *I said My! My! like a spider to a fly. They're dying to add me to their collection!*

The lines at the portable heads are stupendous. Dominique crawls under the platform which booms with sound. As he pisses, tears come to his eyes. He doesn't understand why.

'Why?' Mick says. 'Why shouldn't I?' But the answer doesn't appease his watchdogs. They think it's insane for him to want to *drive* from Houston to New Orleans, *insane!* So many things could happen! Anything could happen . . . after all, this is the *South!* Not Hyde Park! So far everything has gone very well on the tour, but this urge to see the American South in close-up could be a disaster!

'If you think Altamont was something . . .' someone warns.

But the American South is the holy land of rhythm and blues. Why else would Mick have consented to bookings in the concrete and cornporn stadiums of Houston, Mobile and Tuscaloosa? Mick wants to touch the good earth of Dixie. Not as some ridiculous European movie-consciousness, wrought of *Gone With the Wind* and William Faulkner, Erskine Caldwell and Carson McCullers . . . but a profound mystique gleaned from phonograph records, history books and Jagger's own keen intelligence. The South, however, was not visible through the windshield of an expensive automobile any more than it was from eighteen thousand feet. Packaged for tight schedules and imprisoned by security, Mick was the Sleeping Beauty. Brought to his fancy feet every night by the kiss of Prince Peter Rudge. Displayed to the awaiting court and then fondled at a polite distance by the horrendous local heavies, with their proliferated southern dialects and impeccable table manners. Or the perpetually smiling robber-politicians of the South who greeted Jagger with their scathing down-home candour: telling you *everything* they are thinking except the fact that they simply and utterly loathe you.

Then back into the camper and off to a lavishly theatrical dinner at an impersonally gigantic party at a vast and vacuous restaurant. Everybody is angling into position next to the stars, anxious to get in the society page of their catty, local shopping gazette which poses as a newspaper. And then on to the domain of the favoured few – hundred – where you are supposed to rub elbows with the resident *swingers*, those shabby citizens who are in the avant-garde of a society so reactionary that jokes are still made about *Yankees*, *Rebs* and THE UNION. If you're lucky you get laid by somebody new ... or succumb to the incredible tedium of fucking somebody you've been looking through for almost a month. Then sleep.

Mick Jagger clears his throat: 'You don't simply give up all you have ever believed in because you've reached a certain age. Our real followers have moved on with us – but nearly all of them think like us and are questioning some of the basic immoralities which are tolerated in present-day society – the war in Vietnam, persecution of homosexuals, illegality of abortion, drug-taking. We are making our own statement – others are making more intellectual ones. I'm not a spokesman for the immorality of our world. I'm a singer ... a performer. What I do, y'see, is sing. ... But I recognise that there are other inequalities. I know it. The ratio between affluence and reward for work done is all wrong. I know I earn too much, but I'm still young and there's something spiteful inside me which makes me want to hold on to what I've got. But there are things far beyond my hang-ups. In Eastern Europe where they're supposed to set it all straight, the people have *nothing*. All that socialist bullshit. A bunch of gangsters over there. And here in the States too, of course, look at the record industry. Something like Motown which is exploiting blacks like crazy.'

Like somebody said, *Mick has the guile and savvy of a survival artist and the energy and charm of a young advertising vice-president.*

135

Along with that is a keen social awareness and cleverness: an intellect which borders on salon-mentality. Well-informed. Up-to-date. But an intellect which evades the stylishness implied in the salons by denoting a measure of despair and anguish. Mick *knows.* . . . *Gotta scrape that shit right off your shoes.* . . .

It's already dark. And it's 25 July and *Mick Jagger's* birthday concert is the next day, and there hasn't been a word from anybody about Rita's tickets . . . let alone an invitation to the party!

Rita stands silently by the window, the variegated flashes of neon signs tossing her shadow against the wall for a moment and then leaving her in darkness. Then flashing again.

She's crying. But she doesn't understand why. Why it hurts so much. . . . Clawing at her. Pushing at her with the insinuation that *everything* is pointless. That everybody is really as cruel as she's always saying they are. That nobody is really a friend and that the world is just full of bitches. *Bitches* . . . And, well, she can't help it. Being so fucked up. Even enjoying her tears in some perverse way . . . dramatising them. Looking at Brenda Starr who is passed out on the floor with one finger in his mouth and the other one up his ass. Rita meanders over to this chubby graceless body. And as he descends into some kind of passion play, the tears stream down her face. Welling up from the old wound. '*My mother, y'know, she doesn't believe a thing I say. My father tries, but my mother . . . she thinks I'm crazy or somethin'. . . .*' Brenda just moans and pulls in his knees. '*I mean what do these faggots care . . .?*' The party would be such a fab-u-lous event! *My god!* Dylan would be there. . . . *Dylan* . . . And Robbie Robertson. Mick Jagger. Count Basie. Muddy Waters. At the St Regis Hotel . . . *fan-tas-tic! And all kinds of really wild, far-out people! Real stars! Zsa Zsa Gabor and George Plimpton and Woody Allen and Dick Cavett! Even Andy had gotten himself invited . . . but they don't want all his freaks crowding into such a GRAND event! Bitches. . . .*

'Oh, Mama! Can this really be the end? To be stuck inside of Mobile with the Memphis blues again!'

Rita sits on the floor near the couch and flips through his scrapbook, humming quietly and wiping away his tears.

Dominique climbs back on to the stage, feeling stared at and feigning nonchalance. The crew and the Angels begin to get nasty and Dominique shudders at their aggression. He leaps down into the area behind the stage just before a greasy biker reaches him. He sits in the dirt watching as they keep carting off these unconscious bodies. The music rumbles on. The people around him are sitting joylessly, staring at nothing.

'You need somethin' for yah head?' this guy asks Dominique.

'Huh . . .?'

'. . . how about a buck and a half . . . really cheap, man . . . for this little cosmic goodie. A buck and a half . . .'

The guy pushes the tab into Dominique's hand. He opens his palm and stares at it, ripped on grass and tormented by this enormous sob which is hovering just behind his self-control.

The guy is standing over him impatiently. 'A buck then! Shit, man, just give me a fuckin' buck!'

Half-consciously Dominique pulls out a dollar and the kid grabs it and hurries away. Dominique is still staring at the tab . . . a tiny red-orange thing. It doesn't look like the stuff he and Alan used to take. But it could be the same stuff, 'cause, after all, Alan always held the drugs. Alan knew about drugs. And he'd make Dominique open his mouth, saying, *Come on, Dom, don't be a fuckin' drag, man, swallow the thing and let's get our heads fixed up! Man, what's with you, anyway . . . you're always sayin' no no no and then you just fuckin' sail away and nobody can get you back down for three days! So, stop hangin' on to my fuckin' arm and relax!*

'Sure, sure . . . sure. . . .' Dominique whispers as he presses his palm to his mouth and swallows the tab. He taggers to his feet and climbs up on top of a truck where he can see the crowd.

There's a big ugly girl who is rubbing against this guy who has his eyes closed and his arms raised over his head. She keeps taking off her clothes and then, after a while, she stops dancing and crouches down and slowly puts her clothes back on again. Then, a little later, she starts taking them off again.

On stage the Airplane is into 'We Should Be Together'. And there's this enormously obese nude guy with flesh rolling off his hips and chest and shoulders as if he were slowly melting. This large, pale guy ... who is rolling through the crowd like a pinball in slow motion. His flesh-hooded eyes concentrated on the space immediately before them ... inertly. His overstuffed arms outstretched and his fat legs bowed as he lunges to and fro, looking like a giantine baby stumbling recklessly amidst a herd of indifferent dwarfs. On his arm is a tatoo: OSCAR.

By Tuscaloosa the 1972 tour has turned into high tension recapitulation. Jagger stamps out the reactions with utter verisimilitude: the introductions, the smiles and the camp.

The now massive entourage descends upon the Nashville Sheraton shortly after three in the morning following the performance and quick escape from Tuscaloosa that same night. Shortly thereafter the group, having been bivouacked, assembles in the Mezzoriorno – a self-conscious Italian restaurant.

Food and boredom. And a solo violinist who insists upon playing Stones hits until he is quietly eaten alive. Mick wipes his cannibal-mouth and looks entirely unperturbed.

Meanwhile a mob of kids who have been following the tour at a distance are being tossed around like umbrellas at the lost and found by the local authorities. Mac Davis sings about it: *No one wants to help out a long-haired hippie freak at 2 a.m. in Nashville, Tennessee. They threw me out of the truck stop and I got no place to sleep. If this is freedom, lord, it ain't for me. I'm hanging up my Nashville dream as soon as I get home.*

Mick also hangs up his Nashville dream as *The Tongue* leaves Tennessee behind.

For the Old South had died long before – with Faulkner. He foresaw and predicted its decline. He also described the rise of the New South in terms of the rise of the Snopeses. Mick Jagger's artificial paradise and real hell – his image of the South – was the by-product of a whole school of attitudes and postures which reigned majestically in the U.S. during the thirties and forties. But by the time that Jagger arrived to worship at the source, it had vanished under a heavy coat of overly industrialised veneer. The night they drove ole Dixie down. . . .

The South, which had been the agricultural opposite of the northern industrial towns before the Civil War, hung perilously by the impossibility of prosperity through the human use of human beings: slavery. Built around this degenerating precept of labour was a society which increasingly isolated itself from its northern critics and their brutal show of industrial progress. The wealth accrued by the few through the labours of the many was arduously used to broaden the schism between those who were owned and those who owned them. The plantations became the paradox of European refinement in an exploitative social organism. Contrasting the life in the 'big house' was the growth of a folk tradition which blacks forged out of the scraps and garbage of their masters. Nowhere is the love-hate that prevailed among the southern races more evident than in the American music created almost single-handedly by the South. There is an endless borrowing between white and black music. And although Negro styles have moved freely into white music, Negros themselves did not until the great popularity of soul and rhythm and blues.

Prior to the international debut of Chuck Berry and Bo Diddley and the host of black musicians who followed them, the South was eulogised mainly by tribes of white southern kids who had escaped to the cities with their enormous carload of overripe sensibilities. Southern country kids burdened by farm work and isolation have always longed for the bright lights. By the thousands they ventured into Memphis, Nashville, Atlanta and Houston – bringing about the gigantic inertia of a belated and excessive industrialisation of the South.

They brought with them an unmatched treasure of distinctive cultural attitudes: from the isolation of the mountain people, the delta folk and the swamp communities. Among these foundlings was a breed of writer which was unique to America. They produced a decade of a familiar sort of fiction which took the South as its background, terror as its premise, the grotesque as its style, and which used the relations of black and white men as the chief symbol of the problem of evil in our world. Katherine Anne Porter, Carson McCullers, Eudora Welty and Flannery O'Connor were among the special clan of Southern Ladies who emerged. Truman Capote, Tennessee Williams, Jack Dunphy, William Goyen and at least a dozen other male writers grew out of the union of black folklore and homosexual excessiveness: essentially projecting the anti-feminine and decadent elements of Faulkner into a single line of development. Added to this was a prevailing and self-destructive sexual contest between the races. The black woman attained the reputation as the cosmic whore: accessible and rendering pleasure which was free of the guilt of association with white women. The black male became the consummate sexual apparatus: functional, unlimited, mammoth and equally dreaded and desired by repressed white ladies who were saved the defaming of premarital relations by their easy black sisters.

The South which Mick Jagger discovered was the New South: methodically divested of its refinement by the Civil War, of its indigenous music by the commercialisation of the music industry, of its isolation by media, of its vapid virility and unique mythology by the triumph of a dubious equality. The terror was varnished. The grotesque was sanitised. And the southerner was steadily becoming just another American. *The night they drove ole Dixie down. And the bells were ringing and the people were singing* and the core of the racial struggle had dissipated in the North where the real racists lived.

So Jagger turned his back on the dream and was thinking about New York. Meanwhile, D.C. and Norfolk pass in the night. Brittle, hard-driving concerts to curiously deranged audiences. Then Charlotte . . . Toronto. . . .

On 26 July, Rita sat in the darkness of his apartment with his hands over his nose and mouth, staring relentlessly into the air as the hour for the concert approached. Now the remorse in his eyes has been replaced by fear. For if his high voltage delirium is gone . . . if his well-tuned insanity, his camp metabolism has run out. . . . Then there is nothing . . . *nothing*.

No one called and no one came. No one . . . except Brenda Starr. 'Wah . . . Rita, honey . . . ah . . . I mean why doncha just buy a ticket or somethin'. . . .'

'O shut up, Brenda!' Rita had snapped. 'That's not the point, that's not the point, you fucking fool! *Anybody* can buy a ticket! *Anybody!*' And then Rita had murmured, '. . . but when you've waited, y'know, and fought and everything . . . to be a *star* . . . when you think . . . when you feel that maybe . . . that finally they really want you. . . .'

And he shouted: 'THE FUCKING BASTARD PROMISED ME TWO FRONT ROW SEATS IN THE CENTRE! IN THE CENTRE!' Then he pressed the back of his hand against his mouth, softly at first and then violently. '. . . bastard . . .' he muttered, '. . . bastard!'

Now he looks at the telephone. But there's no one left to call. He can't get past a secretary at Atlantic Records. They've heard all the stories. Every story. . . . There just isn't anybody left.

His body feels damp as he sits there staring into the darkness. His breath feels threatened. He's down. Fatally down. *O god, but she is fatally down.* Down down down . . .

He had washed the make-up from his face. *All* of it . . . with a rough washcloth. It left his skin red and blotched. In the mirror, my god, he looked like some ancient man-woman strangling on his obsolescence. Flabbergasted by his terrible impotence. Emptied of starch and strength or any pretense of fortification.

'We're having a good time NOW,' Mick Jagger shouts as the Stones tie up 'You Can't Always Get What You Want'. The Madison Square Garden nation thunders its approval. People are standing on chairs with their arms waving in the air. Just smiling. Miles of smiles!

All except Mark Connelly, that elder master of prose who penned such timely giants as *Beggars on Horseback* and *Green Pastures*, who lifts his eighty-two-year-old body from a second-row-centre seat and turns to leave, telling his trendy friends: 'At least at Jungle Habitat you get to stay inside your automobile!'

The stage crew is swarming around a huge box in which a giant birthday cake is waiting to be offered up to the gladiatorial throng. Mick leaps straight up into the air, and comes down in his semigraceless way on the opening crash of 'Midnight Rambler', and the 1972 tour . . . fifty-four shows in twenty-nine cities . . . is driving at top speed towards its close.

Briiiiiiiiiiiiiiiiiiiiig! It's the bell and Rita leaps up and sobs. Suddenly he sobs! The bell sets off his sobs like an avalanche. These inexplicable sobs. . . . And he can't stop them. *He just can't stop them now!* He holds his hand over his mouth and fumbles for the telephone . . . trying to stop its ringing. incapable of speaking.

BRIIIIIIIIIIIIIIIIIIIIG! The ringing continues even after he lifts the receiver. *BRIIIIIIIIIIIIIIIIIIIIIG!* 'Hello! Hello!' Now he's Blanche DuBois against the wall with her wide, Vivien Leigh-eyes. Mouth opened and about to scream into the telephone: *Fire! Fire! Fire!*

BRIIIIIIIIIIIIIIIIIIIIIIIIIIIG! It's the door. Not the phone! It's been the *door* all this time. And he suddenly begins to laugh. He is laughing and tears are streaming down his cheeks and he opens the door and finds Paco standing there, looking sheepish.

He goes cold and blank. Then he falls back a bit, out of the bright light pouring in from the hallway, and covers his unmade-up face. 'What do you want . . .' he mutters. 'I'm sick. Go away.'

Paco slouches gradually into the room and presses the door closed behind him. Looking like a bad kid. PR confession and absolution. Rita keeps glaring at him as Paco sits in a straight-back chair and looks up through his eyebrows like a cocker spaniel.

'Fuckin' spick bastard!' Rita mutters as he puts the kettle on the stove and reaches under the shower for the stash.

He takes a toke and squats down on top of the truck as Gracie Slick lunges into 'Another Side of Life'. Then a brawl bursts into violence on stage. Dominique stands up but he can't see what's happening.

The music stops.

Then this black guy comes flying out from between the trucks, like he's been thrown off the stage, spitting blood that rolls down his shirtless torso. He's spinning and staggering until he collapses against the truck.

Dominique slides down to the ground, dismayed, and inches towards this wounded black bird. The other people who are standing around look very frightened, staring at the bleeding man but staying their distance. A jacket is passed through the little crowd surrounding him, until someone hands it to Dominique and gestures vaguely for him to give it to the bird. He edges toward the sputtering, furiously suffering man and holds the coat out like he is putting his fingers into the tender fuse of a bomb. The black bird whips its wings and cries out once: KAAAAAAAAAAAAAAAAAA AAAAAAAAH! Then, taking the pea coat into its talons, it whirls imperfectly into the distance. Escaping!

Dominique falls back and tries to focus his eyes. The

Airplane rewinds and starts 'Do Away With People'. But Dominique can't forget the sputtering agony of the black bird as it thundered into the sky. Thrashing the air with his arms like a drowning man. A million bubbles of blood rising from his mouth. *O, my god . . .!* Everything would be fine if Mick Jagger would just come out and SING! Lord, yes, it would be fine if he'd just *sing sing sing singsingsingsing!*

But then thousands of eyes stare at an upraised pool cue. It comes slashing down like a sword. Crashing! Bursting into white water! Hitting the unseen target and sending up a burst of white water. And the huge wave tumbles over the crowd.

The music stops.

Thousands of kids are waving their pathetic V signs.

Dominique sinks back inside the truck and pushes both hands down on the horn as hard as he can. KAAAAAAAA-AAAAAAAAAAAAAAAAAAAAH!!!!! The stage is full of Angels. KAAAAAAAAAAH! OSCAR wheels his enormous body in a circle while people scatter and an Angel brings a pool cue repeatedly down on his shoulders and head. The blood starts slowly. Over the rolls of fat. Melting. OSCAR clutches his wincing body like he is kneading dough. The blood spreads out between his fingers. Slowly.

KAAAAAAAAAAAAAAAAAAAAAAAAAAAAAAAAAAAAAAAAAA-AAAAAAAAAAAAAAAAAH!

'What the fuck is going on . . . !' Gracie Slick shouts over the microphone.

The infernal machine cries out from beneath Dominique's hands. Trumpeting the day of wrath. He falls back and leaps from the truck and rushes headlong into the people sitting between him and the trampled pasture behind the stage.

He falls down and curls up into a ball and waits for the trumpets to stop. *Brian died of a broken heart. Poor Brian. All alone in the water. IN THE DARK DARK water.*

Midnight Rambler. Mick slips off his workshirt to reveal his brilliant glowing white jumpsuit. Six supertroopers dump a shower of crimson light on him. At the Garden the crowd goes wild.

Rita inhales repeatedly, squeezing the haze into his lungs and retaining it there, while he pushes Paco back and pulls his shirt open. Then he unscrews the inhaler and presses it to his nostril, loosening the smog from his lungs while he draws in the Amyl. His large mouth and long plush tongue roam Paco's chest with grotesque eagerness. He pants and salivates and his eyes become bizarre. He's Harold Schartz-berg . . . held captive by the hoodlums of San Bernardino. Shouting while somebody has a hold of his head and is shoving him down.

Gracie Slick can't deal with it anymore. After Marty Balin is knocked out, she falters and her voice changes. Emptied of starch and strength or any presence of fortification. Flab-bergasted by her impotence. '. . . everybody, please cool it,' she says just before an Angel takes ahold of the microphone and tells everybody that *nobody's gonna fuck with his buddies or his bike!*

Mick hams it up. Slinking around while the Garden goes mad. Prancing in the ruby light. Hands on his hips and strutting. Curling his lips, and gesturing with his hands over his head to the band like somebody bringing on a voodoo. Picking up the black rhinestone-studded belt and swinging it around. Swinging it around!

Paco ebbs into a constant purr as Rita tugs awkwardly, trying to get his boyfriend's pants under his hips and down over his legs. But they won't fit over his combat boots . . . the ones with *all* the lacing! So Rita fights with his Levis, standing up and tugging at them while he holds his other arm over his flat naked chest, covering his imaginary breasts. While he salivates and works his large mouth like a woman threading a needle.

Darkness begins to fall at Altamont. Dominique sits up slowly while his head buzzes with twenty-five thousand amps and a colour TV set that's out of focus. For the first time since leaving San Diego, he reaches into the inside pocket of his coat and tries to figure out why he brought his father's pistol. He carefully lays his hand on it. Cuddling it inside his pocket as he sits there. Not even sure if it's loaded. Not even sure if it's true that he's been thinking about using it . . . for protection? . . . on whom? . . . on himself? Mixed up. All mixed up. Not even sure that it's a gun . . . *Not sure*. . . .

Well, now, you've heard about the Boston. . . .
BLAM!!!!!! The belt comes down on the stage as the band hits a monstrous chord.

And Rita cries out as Paco falls on top of her. Jamming down between his skinny, upraised legs. Fondly brutalising his ass. Pushing Rita's legs farther apart and plunging. Obliviously. In his solitary, self-centred rhythm.

'The Stones are here!' somebody shouts, jolting Dominique into focus at Altamont.

'I just saw their helicopter.'

'Sure! . . . look! It's up there . . . sure, can't you see it coming?'

Suddenly the stage lights come on. A wave of hope sweeps the crowd and it presses forward happily until the Angels stride into their midst and glower at them.

Dominique jumps to his feet and begins to run . . . chasing the copter . . . chasing after the black bird which is hovering in the sky as the daylight diminishes and the stage lights throw up a colossal halo. *It's Mick! Jesus, Alan, it's Mick come back to earth on the back of a black bird! It's Mick Jagger! My god, can you believe it, Alan, he's coming down from the sky.*

And as the gusting, whirling bird began to settle into the scrub and chuckholes, Alan smiled at Dominique and said: 'Y'know, that's the *only* guy on earth that I'd step down for. Jagger, y'know, he's really fine!'

That's when Dominique began to cry. That's when he bit down hard on his lips and felt that enormous SHOUT!

which had been tied up inside his chest begin to shatter into sobs.

The copter door opened and the Stones filed out. Dominique reached into his coat pocket and rushed forward, screaming: I HATE YOU I HATE YOU I HATE YOU I HATE YOU I HATE YOU I HATE YOU I HATE YOU I HATE YOU I HATE YOU I HATE YOU I HATE YOU I HATE YOU I HATE YOU I HATE YOU I HATE

Punching Mick in the face with all his might.

BLAM! And the band hits another huge chord.
Talking' 'bout the midnight shhhhhhh
BLAM!
I'm called hit and run raper in anger
And the black rhinestone-studded belt crashes down on the stage again.

As Rita begins to howl softly. Her voice growing louder as her legs wobble and quiver and jostle wildly. And all the time the howl is getting louder and louder.

And Dominique keeps rushing through the crowd, clutching his hand over his breast pocket, manoeuvering endlessly through the people, trying in vain to find an escape. Pale. . . . Dry-mouthed and wide-eyed. While the crowd screams and Mick sings 'Jumping Jack Flash'. And Rita cries out her long long wailing sorrow and pleasure and dread and joy. Oooooooooooooooooooooooooooooooo. . . .

And the Madison Square Garden audience screams when Keith sends a pie into Mick's face. And the whipped cream flies everywhere. And four Angels flash from behind the equipment, tumbling over the stage, snorting and flailing the air with their chunky limbs. And the crowd explodes like egg shells as the Angels roar off the edge of the stage into their midst.

And Dominique keeps running, afraid to look back. And the music stops. 'Fellow, fellow,' Mick is saying, 'move back, won't you, fellow. . . .' And the music starts again. And then more Angels stride into the crowd, beating people back with their pool cues. And there are screams and a chorus of boos as the crowd becomes angry. And the music stops again. And something is going on in front of the stage. Something really terrifying. 'Brothers and sisters ... brothers and sisters ... why are we fighting?'

And Paco throws back his head and cries out and Rita begins to shudder and to yell an endless Ooooooooooooooo-oooooooomygod it's terrible! they hit him ... they hit him I can't tell whether it's with a knife or what but they hit him hard they hit him and everyone screams and falls back and shouts for them to stop stop stop stop stop (*Black - male, medium - height, about - twenty - three - years - old - reaches - into - right - hand - pocket - and - draws - pistol - in - right - hand - raising - it - in - an - angle - perpendicular - to - stage -*) stop stop for godsakes almighty but nobody can stop it now they have him by the arm and they are trying to get something away from him if they can they are trying to get this what I don't know but maybe a gun I'm not sure but it's possible I don't know god I couldn't tell because everyone is pushing and trying to get out of the way in fear that it will go off or maybe the knife I don't know for sure but one of the Angels has a knife I think watch out for godsake watch out watch out watch out (*- stage - as - unidentified - male - Caucasian - medium - height - age - about - twenty - six - years - reaches - with - both - arms - towards - alleged - assailant - towards - gun - and - grasps - arm - in - both - hands - when - second - male - Caucasian - medium - height - age - about - twenty - eight - years - swings - in - 180 - degree - arch - with - what - appears - to - be - sharp - instrument -*) out out out out of the way when he comes running towards me running and staggering and falling forward and everybody clearing out of the way and then he falls falls falls down on his knees and he wavers there and he has his eyes closed and he wavers there there there (*- instrument - and - strikes - the alleged - assailant - in - right - upper - back - the - blade - disappearing - at - forty - five - degree - angle - into - alleged - assailant's - body -*) there there there until the Hell's Angel the same one grabs on to both his shoulders and starts kicking him kicking him in the face and again

and again about five times or more my god and then he falls
down on his face he falls on his face in the dirt and then
and then one of them is kicking him one of them kicking
him on the side and kicks kicks kicks him till he rolls over
and he mutters and some words come out he mutters some
words and he says he says he keeps saying in this mumble
I wasn't going to shoot you I wasn't going to shoot you I
wasn't going to shoot you I wasn't going to shoot you
(- *body - and - assailant - pulls - quickly - away - crouching -
forward - and - rushes - into - the - crowd - immediately - to - the -
left - of - the - assailant - at - the - time - of - the - attack* -) wasn't
going to shoot you and we rub his back up and down we
rub it to get the blood off to try to get all the blood off so
we can see so we can tell if it is terrible so we can see and
there is a big hole oh there is this big hole on his spine right
on his spine God! you know and a big hole on the side and
there is a big hole on his temple on his temple where it's so
soft and sensitive and soft soft soft (- *attack - and - falling -
to - his - knees*) soft a big open slice you could see all the way
in this hole in his temple and you could see you could see
all the way in you could see inside you could see at least an
inch an inch an inch down and the stuff and the stuff stuff
you know the stuff you could see this stuff inside and all of
us we were drenched in blood in blood we were drenched
and this man this poor man he was alive he was living and
breathing he was alive and living just a minute ago we saw
him die and we saw the end of his life and he was alive there
on his knees god in heaven he was on his knees and they
grabbed him god they grabbed him by both shoulders and
they started to kick him kick him again and again and god
again they started kicking him and he opens his mouth and he
opens his mouth and blood starts coming out of his mouth
and teeth my god coming out and he screams he screams
oh god he begins to scream OOOOOOOOOOOOOOOOOOO
OOOOOOOOOOOOOOOOOOOOOOOOOOOOOOOOOOOO
OOOOOOOOOOOOOOOOOOOOOOOOOOOOOOOOOOOO
OOOOOOOOOOOOOOOOOOOOOOOOOOOOOOOOOOOO
OOOOOOOOOOOOOOOOOOOOOOOOOOOOOOOOOOOO

OOOOOOOOOOOOOOOOOOOOOOOOOOOOOOOOOOOOO
OOOOOOOOOOOOOOOOOOOOOOOOOOOOOOOOOOOOO
OOOOOOOOOOOOOOOOOOOOOOOOOOOOOOOOOOOOO
OOOOOOOOOOOOOOOOOOOOOOOOOOOOOOOOOOOOO
OOOOOOOOOOOOOOOOOOOOOOOOOOOOOOOOOOOOO
OOOOOOOOOOOOOOOOOOOOOOOOOOOOOOOOOOOOO
OOOOOOOOOOOOOOOOOOOOOOOOOOOOOOOOOOOOO
OOOOOOOOOOOOOOOOOOOOOOOOOOOOOOOOOOOOO
OOOOOOOOOO-hi-o. Four dead in O-hi-o. Four dead in
O-hi-o! Just a block from beautiful downtown Cleveland
where Rita is painting a large heart on the buttocks of the
Statue of Liberty. And Dominique has to go home for dinner
because it's already half past five. And Alan will be worried.
'Don't be late,' Rita shouts to him. Smiling with her new
breasts and returning to the stove. But, you know, it's
difficult to find a parking place in the kitchen at this time
of night. So everyone is huddled around the sink, having
dry marmosets and talking about Eddie Fisher who was
without a doubt . . . 'Look,' Rita begins to say but decides
to have coffee instead. And Dominique has his hand on his
gun but cannot shoot. So La Senorita Dos Pesos drifts
farther and farther away. And Mick smiles three times and
takes off his shirt and takes off his trousers and takes off his
face and takes off his fingers and takes off the back of his
neck as the lights go out at Madison Square Garden. And
it's quiet. Dominique can hardly hear a soul except for Alan
who has three. And one makes four. 'What is that?' he
giggles as Lyndon Baines Johnson puts his cigar under his
armpit and begins to puff on his stool. And Rita has a
number ten tin can of stewed tomatoes between her legs.
But Paco can't cut the Tomatoes. Just before the Angels of
the Dead come gliding on the wings of black birds. Are
there any more? 'Yes, sir, yes, sir; three bags full. One for
the doctor and *You're under the testicles . . . so get your hands up
or I'll shoot!*' But Paco won't take his repeater off the heater
and Rita can't float. And Dominique begins to run, holding
his hand over his breast penis and dashing into the waves.
Trying to swim around Rita and his flotilla of stars! 'Please,

please get out of the wave!' But Paco won't take his repeater off the heater. Standing there in the nude. '*Please!*' Dominique insists as he staggers further and darker and tries to get over the floating bodies. So many of them! With watery eyes and rags burning in their mouths. 'O my god!' He can't get through! They're pulling him, they're pulling him under! And he is going to pass out as Rita rises into the air and glistens like a star and Judy Garland bursts into tears on the horizon and turns slowly into Marlene Dietrich for just a moment before becoming Mick Jagger and a celestial chorus of girls with glitter in their eyes and big bowed-lips and pink cheeks and powdered bears. And as Richard Milhous Nixon strikes up the band and plays the Mao Tse-Tung March, the assembled dead of Altamont roll over and begin to sing THE SAME OLD PLACES AND THE SAME OLD SONG WE'VE BEEN GOING THERE FOR MUCH TOO LONG THERE'S SOMETHING WRONG AND IT GIVES ME THAT FEELING INSIDE THAT I KNOW I MUST BE RIGHT ... IT'S ... THE ... SINGER ... NOT ... THE ... SONG. ...

smash, 'the meaning ... is ...
between ... the first ... and the second ... word.'

Aftermath

A high, distant scream of interplanetary gas.

Flying at thirty-eight thousand feet above the darkening monotony of the endless Sahara. A continuous visual drone. So repetitious that it turns into something audible. Neither moonscape nor landscape. But rather like something not yet finished or perhaps something which was never begun.

As that world below darkens it also comes to life with sudden, irregular flashes. Countless oil wells exploding into flames. Intermittently the night changes into luminous Hieronymus Bosch. But soon even these surrealistic traces are consumed by the most appalling blackness.

The Boeing time-machine churns out hours of lag. Nothing remains but the unearthed, metallic gliding of this enormous bird. Its constant, electronic song. Leaving deep dark bruises in the mammoth African sky.

But inside the cabin and inside of me the barometer has run dry. Cause is divorced from effect. And the truth about a myth is the myth itself.

Crashing silently through the stratosphere in this imperfect rocket, trying to sleep, I remember the natives of *Mondo Cane* who for the first time saw monstrous planes landing supplies for white soldiers in the midst of their jungle. The natives perfectly misunderstood these logistics and reconstructed an airport of reeds and raffia and sat awaiting the giant bird which would bring food to them too. They had mystified their perfect miscomprehension of what they had seen.

Here we are inside this metallic island, afloat over Africa, and very probably everything we deduce about the sky in which we fly and the earth below and the universe beyond is a similar mystification based upon a similar naïveté.

So it really isn't too unreasonable that we elected Jagger as Satan. The position was available ever since a world of dislocated boy scouts perpetuated the notion that insofar as heaven obviously does not exist perhaps hell is really where it's at. Jagger became the available myth for that vastly innocent notion of evil. Of course, it's a bit like revering an artist because he's rebellious rather than because he's creative. But it fills the need.

I don't want to think about Mick Jagger.

He's probably in New York. Focusing into the ultimate shadow of Fitzgeraldian dandy-hoodlum ... white-suited elegance. With a dildo in his vest pocket. *Très proute ma chère!* Pop-Mafioso! Leader of the pack ... the sensation of *Women's Wear Daily*! A delicate mix of Newcastle rowdy and Edwardian queen. A bit more outrageous every day. *You're so vain I bet you think this song is about you.* . . . . Trucking at the Continental Baths. In and out of all the revolving doors along Park Avenue, Rue de la Concorde, Wijde Heisteeg, Boulevard du Montparnasse. Imitating the people who have turned their imitations of *him* into a movement. Mick Jagger disguised as David Bowie. Bette Davis disguised as Bette Davis. It's all the same trip.

And Bianca. The missing link. On Mick's arm, sailing over the legions of groupies without as much as turning her head. Brimming with *style* ... pants, cane and campy camouflage. Beguiling the courtiers with her elusive etiquette. On her Catholic tightrope, picking her way through all of society's highest places. Balanced upon her stylish exuberance. Coming up from nowhere and suddenly marrying the Satanic Majesty himself ... in a Catholic Church. Combining with Jagger in the magazines and columns. Tumbling directly into the innersanctum. Enthralling hostesses. Becoming the Jackie of rock – reigning with lethal nonchalance. Mick and Bianca smiling the same smile with the same dark face: becoming, on a whim, the couple in centre-stage. In the bright lights!

153

And the airplane lunges into the perfect blackness, and I don't want to think about Mick Jagger.

Two boys hang over the backs of their seats to stare at me. I pretend to be asleep but they begin to speak to me anyway. The blonde one, the American, he saw me on a Chicago TV show. 'You really know Mick Jagger, mistah?'

'Go away.'

The South African kid is going back to school with a pile of Stones albums in his lap. A cultural harpoon which is returning home to Africa by a very long and winding road. Somewhere Bo Diddley is smiling.

'Is Jagger really a queer, mistah?'

But the fact of the matter is that Mick isn't whatever he himself thinks he is. And he isn't what anybody else says he is. If the natural condition of the human body is sleep perhaps the natural transaction of the human brain is illusion.

Boys and girls inherit forty-four chromosomes that determine nonsexual characteristics, plus two sex chromosomes: XY for males and XX for females. *And having written moves on.* . . .

'I got over a hundred caps of acid,' the American kid whispers. 'I'm gonna make out like a bandit at school . . . up to me ass in ice cream!' He's going to sell the LSD to his school chums at six dollars a tab.

He's fourteen years old. He's a wheeler. One of Mick's boys.

He is part of the same tribe which began in 1965 with Emerson, Christ and Buddha and ended roughly at Altamont with Charles Manson, Eldridge Cleaver and B. F. Skinner. Somewhere along the line they joined together the clean extinction of heroin with the stern participation of Maoism. Insisting upon their right to march off into chemical oblivion at the same time that they insist upon the ultimate truth of collective idealism. Sure . . . out in the rice paddies wrecked on smack! Just what Marx had in mind!

So, my friends, we are abandoned here in midair. Riding feebly in the uncertain gust of Mick's last song. Over an ancient jungle. Out beyond the reach of radios and commercials. Hundreds of miles from even the most primitive neon light. But remotest Africa will receive a new stack of Stones albums anyway ... and 100 caps of LSD.

I fasten myself to the black void outside my tiny window. Somewhere out there is some place I haven't seen before. Somewhere out there is life.

But the excruciating complexity of physical science has only recently determined that life, in its most basic components, is strangely *simple*. So simple, in fact, that it occurs with great ease and regularity *everywhere*. A very basic premise of Western man has been upset, even outraged, by this discovery.

Mick Jagger reflects this dazzling destruction of the sentimental *idea* of life. And he suggests something profoundly simple in its place: Despite the meekness and complacency of human life, man finds infinite power in the experience of himself. Though he appears to be insignificant in the scope of things, though he is smaller than he ever dreamed, he is still awed by his own divinity and by the enormity of his *feelings*.

Mick Jagger celebrates these *feelings*. He transforms the ineffable, stupendous urge of the living into virtual images of life itself. He coaxes rapture from the energy of gospel meetings. He entices beauty from the banalities of the herculean innocence of American commerce. From the primordial white rites of Johnny Ray and Elvis Presley to the kidnapped disorder of Africans like Dobie Gray, whose grandfather was shipped C.O.D. to the Mississippi delta. Silt in the mouth of the river.

But the muddy water which I see is only a reflection in my window. There is no trace of land or river from this stratospheric ride. I have been up too long and I want to come down.

'But when my mind is free,' Dobie cries, 'y'know a melody can move me, and when I'm feelin blue, the guitar's comin thru to soothe me.' Singing along with these words of Mentor Williams: 'So thanks for the joy you've given me ...

155

I want you to know I believe in song . . . rhythm rhyme and harmony. They've helped me along; they're makin me strong. So gimme the beat boys and free my soul! I wanna get lost in your rock and roll . . . and drift away.'

SONG AND DANCE MAN

MICHAEL GRAY

'The best Dylan study yet – with massive quotation from his lyrics and a careful balance held in assessment of his work.'
Sunday Times

75p Illustrated

ELVIS

JERRY HOPKINS

'Just about as comprehensive a book as anyone is ever likely to offer on a pop idol. This is exactly the book which legions of Presley fans throughout the world will clamour for.'
Evening News

£1·00 Illustrated

JOHNNY CASH

Winners Got Scars Too

CHRISTOPHER S. WREN

A fascinating biography which traces Johnny Cash's career from his boyhood on an Arkansas farm during the Depression to his current eminence as the king of country music.

60p Illustrated

POETRY DIMENSION 1

Edited by JEREMY ROBSON

The first truly comprehensive look at the current poetry scene, which highlights the best poetry and the best prose about poetry published in books and magazines over the past twelve months.

75p

THE PARADE'S GONE BY ...

KEVIN BROWNLOW

The classic and acclaimed work on Hollywood during the 'golden age' between 1912 and the advent of sound sixteen years later.

£1·75 Illustrated

STANLEY KUBRICK DIRECTS

ALEXANDER WALKER

Richly illustrated with over 350 stills, which add force to the detailed analyses of style and content, this book traces the flow of Kubrick's work from *Paths of Glory* to *Dr Strangelove, 2001: A Space Odyssey*, and *A Clockwork Orange*.

£1·00 Illustrated

GETTING BACK TOGETHER

ROBERT HOURIET

'A charged and comprehensive report on American communes
that is also an odyssey, one man's confession . . . It's difficult not
to be moved.'
Cosmopolitan

75p Illustrate

THE BOOK ON THE TABOO AGAINST
KNOWING WHO YOU ARE

ALAN WATTS

'This lovely and humorous work will shock, outrage, excite,
delight and profoundly stimulate anyone who has ever asked
"Who or What am I?".'
Irish Press

45p

BLACK ELK SPEAKS

The Life Story of a Holy Man of the Oglala Sioux as told to JOHN G. NEIHARDT

'A beautiful and eloquent testament to the dream of a way of life
that died with a people in defeat.'
The Cork Examiner

90p Illustrated

EARTH IN UPHEAVAL

IMMANUEL VELIKOVSKY

'Velikovsky abandons the literary and the legendary. He goes into the fields of astronomy, archaeology, geology and biology . . . to cast serious doubts on all kinds of accepted hypotheses in these various fields.'

Diogenes, Time and Tide

60p

AGES IN CHAOS

IMMANUEL VELIKOVSKY

Dr Velikovsky reconstructs the political and cultural histories of the nations of the ancient world to present a unique and radical revision of ancient history.

75p Illustrated

THE VIEW OVER ATLANTIS

JOHN MICHELL

A revolutionary theory of prehistoric civilisation, already established as an 'underground' classic.

75p Illustrated